Our Girl

John Rich Dorean

Merry John Press

Jefferson, Pennsylvania

ISBN 978-0-9851994-3-2

By the same author

The Kingdom Adventure
Murder in Greene
Witness in Greene
Justice in Greene

Dedicated to the family of Christ with whom I have
shared ministry at the Jefferson Baptist Church for
more than thirty-five years, who have truly embraced
the reality that Beth is Our Girl, and to the medical
community of doctors, surgeons, physician assistants,
nurses, therapists, technicians and aides who have
been a part of God's sustaining presence in Beth's life

PREFACE

This book is an attempt to chronicle, describe and reflect on the life to date of our youngest daughter, Bethany. Though my name appears on the cover and title page, the book is, in fact, co-written. I, John, have written the narrative found in these pages, but their core content is based in large measure on the yearly journals that my wife and life partner, Merry, has kept since very near the beginning of Bethany's life. Without those journals, the story could never have been told for they are essential to virtually every paragraph found here.

We are both incredibly indebted to three ladies, Carol Scott, Joey Sieg-Tom and Greta Acklin, all very good friends, who have proof read and edited the original manuscript for us, not only providing important grammatical corrections, but adding suggestions for significant revisions which we feel have strengthened the book. As with my three earlier mystery novels, we owe a huge debt of gratitude to friend and brother in Jesus, Allen Fox, for doing all of the tedious work of layout. Our daughter, Carrie, has once again done all of the work on front and back covers and like her sisters, Emily and Hannah, has offered her amazing love to thirty years of caring for Beth.

And words cannot begin to express our thanks to the people of the Jefferson Baptist Church and the broader Greene County community for the beyond belief support, encouragement, and love they have offered us through the days that have become decades with our girl. Incredibly, we are now a family of eighteen when we all gather for Christmas or summer vacation. Spread over three states and the District of Columbia, our four daughters, three sons-in-law and nine grand children are a blessing we could only dream of and pray for when this story begins. Thirty-five years as the pastor of a little church in Jefferson, PA was also little more than a dream and a prayer in the early days of Beth's life.

We had left six and a half years of life in the Christian community of Koinonia Farm in southwest Georgia, where we had met and begun our family, in January, 1982, and began life as a pastor and family five months later. Our hearts and minds were filled with grand ideas of serving God's Kingdom and people in ways that would radically transform this place where God planted us. But four short years later, the birth of our fourth daughter would instead radically transform us. That's the story told in these brief pages.

Table of Contents

Table of Contents

CHAPTER ONE

The First Days July 1986

WE ARE THE parents of a rather remarkable thirty year old young woman. Beth's life has been extremely fragile since birth. When we were sent home after six weeks in the neonatal intensive care ward at Mercy Hospital in Pittsburgh, we were told that she likely would not live six months. We were convinced that the Mercy doctors were sending her home to die and, frankly, we were terrified that she would not survive the car ride home.

Fear: that was to become a very big part of our lives in those early years. My wife Merry had actually known some fear in the final months of her pregnancy with Beth. When I say that, it is important that you understand that my wife is not the fearful type. She is the one who climbed high into the tree to attach a rope swing for our daughters and the local kids. She is the one who worked hours every day in the community garden in southwest Georgia like the mythical slave woman, with our eldest daughter, Emily, secured in a pack on her back.

And this was our fourth child: the first delivered in a birthing center, the second by a granny midwife and the third at home with no one present but our four year old daughter, Carrie. (Merry had sent Emily to the neighbors for help and I was off doing my pastoral thing at a couple of community meetings, in the days before the ubiquitous cell phone.) Merry loved being pregnant, loved birthing children, was born to be the great Mom and Grandma that she is. No, fear was not a part of her makeup.

But she feared during the months of her pregnancy with Beth. She had taken a dip in a hot tub before she knew she was pregnant and worried that that might have caused her growing baby harm. She did not feel the baby move and kick as much as her other three had done. We prayed, visited a lay midwife regularly and went about life. That first taste of fear from my usually confident wife should have gotten my spiritual attention more, but it did not.

The truth is I was probably a little cocky about this baby thing. Merry was a natural mom; she loved everything about it. She comes from a family of eight kids and the four girls, like their mother before them, were prolific producers. I pretty much only had to look at Merry for her to become pregnant. And her grit and determination in the birth process was remarkable. Giving birth was what women had done for thousands of years. It was what Merry had done well three times before. She/we could handle anything.

And then July 13, 1986 rolled around and Bethany Maria Dorean came into the world in the very early morning hours. As with the birth of daughter number three, Hannah, this delivery moved rapidly. Merry had felt her contractions begin and had later called the lay midwife who was to assist. She

2

arrived sometime after Beth was delivered. As it turned out, totally unknown to us ahead of time, Beth was a breech birth. We would find out days later that her left leg was broken coming though the birth canal. But when that butt dropped out before the head, we flew into a panic, sending eleven year old Emily to read aloud the emergency birthing book. Before she got to the section on breech births, Beth was out and snuggling at her mother's breast.

She became pale when she nursed so Merry had to stop nursing pretty frequently. We noticed that if we touched her leg she would cry and that worked to get her color back. Otherwise she made no sound. After a few minutes we decided all was not well and called the local fire department's ambulance service to take her to the hospital. But in the few minutes it took for them to arrive, she seemed to improve and so when they came and checked her out, we decided not to go. That was our decision, not theirs, and one which in hindsight was probably a mistake. But what it meant was that we got to spend several hours together at home as a family before the medical ordeal that was to consume much of the next fifteen years or so began. It may also have contributed to that ordeal. But that's one we won't know for sure, in this life at least. Everyone got to hold her and those hours of Merry holding Beth skin to skin would be the last any of us would have to hold her for weeks.

A good friend and prayer warrior, Marie Simmons, who had arrived with me several minutes after Hannah had been born, came again this time and prayed with us. And the midwife arrived, did an exam and left thinking all was well (or at least OK.) We all tried to sleep. But by 6:30 A.M. we decided we needed help.

We had been in Jefferson four years by then, but none of us had been to a doctor. We had decided after Emily that we did not want to go the traditional route of vaccinations for the girls and all of us were in remarkably good health. We knew, by name only, of Dr. Eric Stacher, a local pediatrician, and gave him a call. Huge credits go to the man for taking a call at 6:30 A.M. on a Sunday morning from folks he had never heard of before. After listening to our description of the situation, he agreed to meet us at the local hospital in half an hour.

I had to scurry to get folks to cover for me in the church service that would soon be upon us. Graciously, a good friend and retired LPN, Alice Kramer, agreed to go to the hospital with us. When we got there, Merry and Alice went with Bethany to one of the exam rooms and I went to the registration desk to check us in.

When I came back from that process, nurses pointed me to the exam room where Merry and Beth were both being checked out. Before I got to the door, Alice came out and said, in a voice filled with concern, "John, it doesn't look very good for the baby." I had no idea what she meant, and truth be told, I don't think she had a clue as to what lay ahead for all of us. I asked, "What do you mean, Alice?" To which she replied, "Well, she has club feet and maybe some other issues."

Again with an arrogant confidence in the wonders of American medicine, I quickly reasoned that club feet could be handled easily enough with a few surgeries. And though this might mean that Beth would not be going to the high school pool to swim at the age of two weeks like Hannah had done, still there was not a real fear of what might await her or us.

As I opened the door, there before me stood a man of about my age in a bright red Mickey Mouse shirt, a Pennsylvania State Police ball cap and gold chains on his neck and wrists.

He took one look at me and said, "Are you the father?" And I blurted out, "Are you the doctor?" His attire belied his ability.

While it would be weeks before we would begin to get a handle on all that was wrong with Beth, Dr. Stacher moved with cool efficiency to put her on oxygen and began to have her fed with Merry's milk through an NG tube. She was then quickly whisked away to be admitted to the hospital neo-natal unit. For those used to a big city neo-natal unit, think severe downsize. In fact, the very small, maybe 80 square foot glassed in room in which Beth would spend the next three days was the unit. But she was placed in an incubator and nurses began the arduous task of trying to tube feed her.

We would only find out weeks later that Bethany had a motor neuron related disease that left her with something like one-tenth of the muscle tissue of the average human. That showed up in a variety of ways, but one of the first we were to notice with real concern was her inability to swallow well. It would be a while before anyone realized that she was in fact aspirating some of her food into her lungs. And equally troubling was her inability to keep food down. She was prone to reflux much of what she ate. That would soon cause other crisis-producing problems. But for the moment, getting enough food in her to sustain life was a real concern.

Three nurses (again think small hospital) took on the round the clock effort to get fifteen cc's of breast milk (Merry was pumping from day one and continued for the next nine months) down her tube every two hours. If they went too fast, she would bring it all back up. The patience and care those ladies brought to that effort and their tender care for Beth and all of us remains, thirty years later, treasured in our hearts.

Back in Jefferson, the deacons had had a time of prayer and a brief hymn sing and dismissed church early. Soon we were being surrounded by friends both from our church family and others from my Mom's church in Waynesburg. We felt incredibly supported and knew that prayers were being lifted up for us all throughout the country.

Friends in Georgia called friends in Florida who left us a message on our home phone that we got that first evening encouraging us to pray boldly, to trust God completely and to not go to the hospital. Had we gotten that message before we went, going would have had an element of guilt that it did not have. We have always believed that God is the source of all healing and have relied on Him in prayer. But we have only occasionally trusted Him to the exclusion of medical assistance, with mixed results.

Friends from both our church family and my mom's (First Presbyterian) began that first night to bring us meals. They would continue that selfless practice for months on end. At one point the deacons from First Pres came and said, "We would like to discontinue the meals now." To which we responded, "Please, no, we need them so badly." And they continued on several more months.

While obviously we had no idea what lay ahead of us as a family, that first day began our adaptations to a forever changed existence as caretakers of Bethany. We also started what would become the daily shuttles to and from the hospital, one of us going home for food and shower, returning with the three girls and then staying while the other got a turn at home.

Early kudos to Beth's three sisters whose lives were from that day forward robbed of a lot of the ease and comfort that they had known up until then and that a lot of kids in America take for granted. From that moment on for the next six weeks and for much of the next two years, they would rarely see their parents together, except in the hospital. While certainly knowing nothing of the pain of families separated by death or divorce, our girls bore a tremendous emotional and spiritual burden. We knew it, wished it weren't so, but there was simply no way to avoid it.

We continued to homeschool Emily and Hannah that first year with Beth. Remarkably those two kept their focus and stayed up with their studies with all that went on around them. With Merry spending most days in the hospital and me trying to maintain a full work schedule, our oldest, Emily, ended up doing a lot of instruction for Hannah. As the years went by, the girls all ended up going to public school and turned out to be very successful student athletes. All three of them became teachers.

Both Merry and I have kept a log in one form or another of what happened through the course of the day since the day of Beth's birth. On July 15, the third day of Beth's life with us, Merry, writing to Beth, notes, "Dad sings, 'In my life, Lord, be glorified...' today. We sing all the songs we can think of to you."

And it is true. We sang then and we still sing to and with Beth. She has a love for music that is really quite special. For years a favorite song in the family and larger church family was "Make Me a Servant." And for reasons unknown to any of us, Beth would break into tears every time it was sung.

The four days a week that I get her fed and showered in the morning, she always asks about half way through the prep time, "Is it too early to sing, Daddy?" (It has become a ritual of sorts and interestingly it is the only time she ever calls me "Daddy.") To which I have always responded, "It's never too early to sing." And she will break into one of the many Broadway tunes or hymns that we routinely sing, the louder the better as far as we are both concerned.

Music, and especially music that brings praise to God, has been an effective weapon in battling through the temptation to discouragement or depression throughout Beth's life. Like reading the Word of God, praise has consoled and encouraged us with great regularity.

One of those first nights, sitting just outside Beth's room, reading my old Revised Standard Version Bible that my brother, Tom, had made a leather cover for years earlier, I came across this verse that has radically altered my understanding of the events of Beth's life and many others like her. **Deuteronomy 29: 29 The secret things belong to the Lord our God. But that which is revealed belongs to us and to our children that we may do all the words of the law.**

The secret things belong to the Lord our God. We wish it were not so, we wish that we had special insight, an ability to see the meaning and purpose behind the stuff that goes on in our lives. How much easier it would be to bear the hard things of life, we reason, if we could know the whys behind it all.

9

Trust me, I have wondered hundreds of times why God gave us three beautiful, intelligent daughters who are really good athletes and then gave us Bethany who, at age thirty, cannot read or add or scribble anything much more than her name and has never walked a step in her life, never caught a ball unless it was pretty much dropped in her lap. What eternal purpose does it serve to have her spend her life lying on a gurney or cruising in her power chair rather than running races or shooting hoops or batting a softball like her sisters? I feel as if life would be so much more manageable if I could see His plan behind Beth's suffering, or the other girls' health.

As I was writing the early chapters of this book, two of our daughters were seated in the VIP section of the Boston Marathon of 2013. They were watching a good friend run the race and were cheering her on directly across the street from The Forum. Just about nine minutes after they left their seats to congratulate their friend, when they were safely a block away, two bombs went off that killed three and injured a hundred and forty innocent people. I weep thinking about God's mercy to us in getting them out of harm's way, even as I weep for those who were not shown that same mercy. Why some and not others? God is all powerful or He is not God at all. He could have saved them all. But he chose not to. How come?

The secret things belong to the Lord our God. It is not for me to know the reasons why, not for me to understand the eternal plans and purpose of God. Yeah, sure, I'd like to know. But He is not letting me in on the secret. And sorry, He is not letting you in on it either.

I think some Christians don't get that. They think that if they put a lot of work into their relationship with God, praying a lot, reading their Bibles a lot, God is going to let them in on those secret things. C.S. Lewis describes life as a maze of train tracks at a major city station. From the ground, it is utterly impossible to tell where each of the intersecting tracks will lead. Only from the control tower can the engineers make sense of the maze and direct the various trains with different destinations to their proper locations. Lewis says that we think that God should invite us up into the control tower. Alas, He does not.

I have been to Haiti on five mission trips and hope to go again. Inevitably, at some point, before, during or after the trip, it occurs to me to ask why the grace of God was shown to me and my family to be born in the United States of America and not in Haiti. It certainly does not have anything to do with my deserving that grace. I have met many devout Christian people in Haiti whose endurance and bright spirit through incredibly challenging times put any faith of mine to shame. How come I get to be raised in prosperity and relative security and those born in Haiti, by no fault or decision of their own, are relegated to such poverty and suffering? I don't get it.

The secret things belong to the Lord our God. But that which is revealed belongs to us and to our children that we may do all the words of the law. Here's what that says to me: I do not, will not in this life, know why Beth was born the way she was born, why the other girls were born the way they were born. But God has shown me, in His word and, I would say, through the common grace of life itself, what it means for me to be a good father to all four of my daughters. And He expects me to do that.

I am slow in a lot of ways, not the least of which is in picking up spiritual insight. So sometimes God has to "reveal" it to me real plainly. Here's how the lights went on for this one.

I mentioned the nurses at Greene County Memorial working so diligently to get fifteen cc's of food down Beth every two hours. Well, that pattern continued for about six months. Because she did not move much at all and did not breathe deeply (more results of the muscle weakness) she quickly became congested and required percussion therapy to prevent pneumonia. We would do fifteen minutes of that (we called it "pounding") before settling into trying to coax her food down her. The feedings often took thirty minutes or more. So forty-five minutes of every two hours twenty-four hours a day was taken up with feeding and percussion therapy. That did not include the usual details like bathing, changing diapers, holding the baby.

So we worked around the clock on four hour shifts. I was, of course, trying to maintain a regular work load at the church while Merry was carrying on care for the household and homeschooling two of the other three girls. Do I need to tell you that after several months of that we were just flat out exhausted? I found myself thinking about doing this another two weeks, another two months, another two years. And one night in the wee small hours of one of my four hour shifts, I broke down sobbing.

"I just can't do it anymore," I muttered to myself.

And without an audible voice, yet as clearly as if it had been one, I sensed God saying to me, "Can you do one more round of percussion therapy?"

"Well, yeah, I can do one more."

"Then do it. Can you do one more feeding, change one more diaper?"

"Yeah, I can do that."

"Then do it. That's what being a good father to Bethany means for you right now."

I think the fundamental principles of AA and NA have a lot to teach all who struggle with long term health issues or, for that matter, long term sin issues. Take it one day, maybe one hour at a time. We will only drown in the impossibility of it all if we fixate much beyond that.

If someone had told me back in those early weeks and months with Bethany that I would still be changing her diapers thirty years later, I would probably have done myself or her in, or left my family, or something equally extreme. And that is not said with some intention of shocking anyone. I think it's the truth.

A line of the Lord's Prayer has become increasingly important to me. "Give us this day our daily bread." I pray that this way, as I pause at each phrase of the prayer. Give us all that we need: physically, emotionally, and spiritually. And give it today. I will trust you for it tomorrow."

We are all so tomorrow driven, knocking ourselves out to make enough money for tomorrow, socking away every spare cent in retirement accounts for tomorrow, insuring ourselves against tomorrow. I don't want to be irresponsible, but the same God who provided for us today will be there to provide for tomorrow. The same God who saw us through those first hours with Beth will see us through the next thirty years.

We worry that He who has never been unfaithful will suddenly change His pattern of all eternity and in our one

13

instance be unfaithful. Instead we ought to focus on being faithful to Him today and trusting Him for tomorrow.

***

Chapter Two

The Next Five Weeks 1986

IT WAS AT about the end of the third day at Greene County Memorial that we really had the first sense of just how serious Beth's condition was. Thanks to the incredible diligence of those three nurses, feedings were going OK, the oxygen in her incubator was keeping her color good and, though she still didn't move much and slept a whole lot, we were already slipping into something of a benign routine.

Then, about 9:00 P.M. on Tuesday night, an orthopedic surgeon whom Dr. Stacher had been asking to do a consult showed up and dropped a bombshell. He was the first to determine that Beth's left leg was broken. But he also concluded that she had a form of arthrogryposis, a stiffening of the joints. Beth's lack of muscle tissue makes her incredibly floppy in all of her limbs, but for reasons we never fully understood, (like maybe lack of movement in the womb?), she has stiffness in some joints. It was an incomplete diagnosis, a less than accurate diagnosis, but it set a whole new world in motion.

He recommended immediate transfer to a more sophisticated facility. To this day we are not sure what the rush was. But quite literally in the middle of the night a team of residents from Mercy Hospital (where Dr. Stacher had done his own residency years prior) swooped down upon us and the medical community of GCMH.

Through the years we have learned that everything seems darker, weightier, more frightening in the night, even within the safe confines of a fully lit hospital. Fear reigned in our hearts. Again for reasons unknown, residents took Merry and me into separate rooms and recorded a history of the last three days. While we were desperate to tell them anything and everything that we thought might help our daughter, there was suddenly a state of almost panic in our hearts. Though I am quite certain that it was not intended as such, the fact that we were questioned separately gave us both the feeling of being interrogated. Had we done something wrong that was going to be used against us somehow?

That thought had been planted in both of our minds on the first day in the hospital when a nurse, who has since become a good friend, made a disparaging comment about the irresponsibility of people who do home births. But her tune changed radically within twenty-four hours when she read a column by none other than Erma Bombeck. The article had "coincidentally" appeared in Monday's paper and talked about the special quality of those whom God has entrusted with special needs children. She apologized for her judgmental attitude, but the seed of having done wrong was planted.

While the "interrogation" was going on, others of the Mercy team were prepping Beth for the trip. And, apparently satisfied that they had gotten everything they could from us, the team prepared to take off for Pittsburgh. We were totally unprepared for such a parting. Merry was allowed to travel with the team, sitting in the front seat of the ambulance. She has often spoken about how terrible that ride was, as she could hear and see the residents working with Beth, but was not allowed to go back and comfort Beth with her touch.

As for me, my last moments with my newborn baby before she was whisked away to the big city were walking beside her incubator as it was wheeled down the hallway to the waiting ambulance. I swear Beth's eyes never left mine as she looked up with terror written in every aspect of her countenance. The muscle weakness left her in those early days and weeks unable to make a sound, but her eyes wailed with fear.

"Do something, Dad," they seemed to scream. "Don't let them take me away," even as she was loaded into the ambulance and sped to Mercy. I was left sobbing uncontrollably, unable to do anything but return to my home and my three sleeping daughters.

And so it began, the daily trips to Pittsburgh. Merry was at Mercy those next five weeks more than she was away from it. Often she would ride to Pittsburgh with a good friend, Martha Noftzger, who was in med school at the time, and I would go up with the girls in the evening for a brief visit and to give her a ride home.

Merry's mom came from her home near Philadelphia to help out at home and stayed about eleven days. Other family members came to help out and to visit. Merry's Uncle Bill came all the way from North Carolina, on several occasions staying for weeks at a time, and baked bread for us and the neighborhood. He was an enormous help in keeping things somewhat stable at home. And Merry's sister, Louise, came and actually took the other three girls to her home outside of Philadelphia for nine days. The support we got from family and friends was an incredible gift from God that sustained us through all the turmoil. I cannot begin to imagine how folks survive such an ordeal without that kind of love lifting them up.

Life did go on. Merry's journal notes that Carrie won the Rain Day Umbrella Contest that July and mine notes that I performed two weddings in those first two weeks of Beth's life. One Tuesday we all took a few hours and snuck off to Kennywood (the local amusement park) together, before going into the hospital to see Bethany. While our hearts and minds were never far from our little girl in Mercy, we all did our best to do what had to be done to keep the whole family flourishing.

Some days I would spell Merry in our vigil over our precious baby. Some nights were spent in recliners in a less than pleasant waiting room outside the neo-natal ward.

Merry longed to try to nurse Beth. Nursing had been a precious, almost holy bond with her first three, and it ripped at her heart to not be able to do it more for number four.

We, one or the other of us, were there every day, though sometimes we might only get to be with her for a few hours or maybe only a few minutes in the course of the day. On July 30, Merry notes in her journal, "Mom held you for twenty minutes today." I cried when I read that. The thought that she was there for at least eight hours and got to hold this precious baby girl for only twenty minutes seems so sad. But that's the way it was.

Any time there was a shift change, we were kicked out while report was being given. Anytime there was any kind of emergency with any one of the children in the unit, we were kicked out. And anytime they were doing anything much at all with Bethany, we were kicked out.

The best times were when all was pretty stable with her and we could sit in one of the big rocking chairs and hold her while we rocked. The NG tube was always hanging from her nose and an IV attached at her wrist. Bright lights were always glaring, but the special bond of parent and newborn child nestled together was never diminished. Maybe a nurse or a resident would come by and we could talk with them about their perceptions about what was going on with our little one.

One night Merry was allowed to nurse. The nurse on duty, having no way of calculating how much food Beth had received, insisted on also tube feeding her. It was simply too much for those weak stomach muscles. Beth aspirated and very nearly died. She refluxed her food and (again because of the muscle weakness) was unable to get it all the way up and out and breathed it into her lungs. That almost choked her to death and left her with pneumonia. Poor Merry went through that one alone, left outside the unit while our girl was whisked away to the surgical floor to be scoped.

When I saw her next, it was a shocking experience. She had lost weight so her head was thinner and her beautiful dark hair was now shaved so that an IV could be placed in her scalp. Another result of the muscle weakness, Beth's veins are very small and difficult to find. To this day, she remains a very difficult stick even for those who have done IVs for years.

The change in her appearance was so drastic that I was convinced, and I still joke about it, that they had switched babies on us. She looked so pale and sickly. (When her hair came back in it was blond, further convincing me of the switch. Ah, the ridicule I have received from my family for such a thought.) The incident certainly intensified our awareness of how incredibly fragile Beth's health was.

Throughout those weeks in Mercy, the search for a more accurate diagnosis intensified. Many of her symptoms mimicked those of muscular dystrophy, and for a while some of the doctors were leaning towards that conclusion. Whether her condition was stable, or likely to get better, or possibly worse, became a part of the equation that we had not given any thought to. I know that I had thought that she would get well, by which I meant, be like our other three daughters, running and playing and enjoying life. That was certainly the focus of my prayers.

I should probably say a word about my prayer life at this time. I have never been a great prayer warrior, was not then, am not now, do not expect that I ever will be. That said, I believe strongly in the power of prayer. I have never been one who subscribed to the name it and claim it school of prayer, never felt inclined to join the health and wealth folks who think that God is sitting around in heaven just waiting to hear from us to shower us with material blessings of every size and shape.

To some, that confession will leave me practically an unbeliever. So let me say again that I believe strongly in the power of prayer. Today I would probably say that my prayer life is largely centered around glorifying God for who He is and what He does and in trying to reshape my life more completely into His image.

In those early days with Beth, I was as close to being a firm believer in "faith healing" as I likely ever will be. Years earlier, we had prayed one night when Carrie had a fever of 104 degrees and was lying limp in her bed. Five minutes later, her temperature was gone and she was up running around the room. You call it what you want, explain it however you choose. I saw it and believed all the more in God's ability to hear and answer prayer.

So, yeah, I prayed that Bethany would be healed, by which I meant made "normal." I have since wondered if we have a clue what normal is, wondered if in many ways Beth is not a whole lot more like Jesus than the rest of us with all our petty issues that she has never even considered.

21

I also ought to confess that there were a lot of times in those early years when I was just too weary, emotionally and spiritually as much as physically, to pray. And in those times I was so very, very grateful to know that people all over the country were praying for her in my stead, praying for me and my family. I may spend most of my early days in heaven just thanking folks for those prayers.

Teams of doctors with a variety of specialties began to check on Beth on a daily basis: gastro-enterologists, neurologists and pulmonologists. And each wanted to run his/her own tests to determine what more could be done for her.

So one day we got sent to Children's Hospital of Pittsburgh, a name that rings with almost holy reverence in the hearts and minds of most folks in western Pennsylvania. Beth was to get an EMG there. Consider yourself blessed mightily by the Almighty if you and your loved ones are spared that procedure. It basically involves sticking needles in just about every part of the human body and an electrical shock applied to measure the reaction. Think the cells in Gitmo; think water-boarding; think torture. I am not sure which was worse, the needles and the shocks that Beth endured, or having to watch it being done to your kid. Remember she could not utter a sound because of the muscle weakness, but she was screaming with every ounce of her body.

One can only wish there was something redemptive about it all. You know, Jesus goes to the Cross, dies an excruciatingly painful physical death and, far worse, experiences the isolation from and abandonment by His Father for the sin of all the earth that has ever, will ever be done. No one has ever suffered as He did. But the salvation of all who put their faith in Him resulted from it. At least something good came of it.

I never did see anything good from that EMG. I was ready to strangle the neurologist who went right along with his test seemingly oblivious to the pain it was causing our daughter.

We later learned that he was one of the best in the country at his craft, but that did little to console me. It would be weeks before we would get his report.

Before then, the folks at Mercy were bent on shipping us home. It seemed to happen kind of all at once. We had settled into something of a routine, but I can't say that I ever felt we were making much progress. Folks seemed less sure of a diagnosis than when we arrived. Beth's health was as fragile as it had been when we arrived, maybe more so since she had

had repeated episodes of aspiration. The staff of doctors and nurses in the unit were wonderfully kind to us all, but never really hinted that our time with them was about up. I guess we should have figured that out.

But one day they announced that Merry and I needed to get trained in CPR and as soon as we had a quick tutorial, they were loading us up and saying goodbye. And we were off at that aforementioned trip home when we were sure she was going to die. As it turned out, she was fine and so were we, all relatively speaking, of course.

I remember thinking at the time that we would, all of our lives, stop back and visit that unit and folks would marvel with us at how far Beth had come. I thought someone would probably write a newspaper article on the relationship of our family and the unit's staff over the years. We actually did stop back once, only a few weeks after we left, and could only find one person who even vaguely remembered us. So much for that article.

But we grew in confidence as daily we learned to know what Beth needed most in her care and we grew in our confidence to give it to her. Within a year I would write an article for a national magazine entitled, "The Parent as Nurse, Respiratory Therapist and Surgeon?" But before that we would be introduced to a man who shaped our lives forever and who, next to God Almighty, we give the most credit for getting Beth and all of us where we are today.

***

CHAPTER THREE

A New Beginning September 1986

H ERE'S HOW HE came into our lives. At the time we had an insurance company that was run by the Ministers and Missionaries Benefit Board of the American Baptist Churches USA. They were an incredible organization to work with and cared for us like no agency since. After a while (it seemed to us that it was probably due to the cost of Beth's care) MMBB discontinued being the direct insurer. But in those early days of Beth's life, they were phenomenal.

Shortly after we returned home, they sent us a health care coordinator who in about two visits changed our lives. She recognized from the get-go that, since we had been released from Mercy's care, we were flitting from one specialist to another with no one to provide oversight for Beth's care. The neurologist was doing his thing, the gastroenterologist doing his, the respiratory folks their thing and nobody was looking at the whole picture of Beth's life.

So our coordinator did some research and came back with a recommendation that we go to Children's Hospital to see

Dr. Basil Zitelli. There was a part of us that was thinking, "All we need is one more doctor." But at the very same time a good friend of Merry's, who lived in the Boston area and had a special needs child of her own, asked her doctor from Children's Hospital of Boston whom he would recommend we see. And he offered up the same name, Dr. Basil Zitelli. An appointment was made and our lives forever blessed.

When we first arrived, we were shown directly into Dr. Zitelli's office, not an exam room. For those familiar with the new Children's Hospital of Pittsburgh, it may be hard to picture, but this room was crowded and not particularly well-lit. The only window faced another part of the building just a few feet away. Bethany had one of her choking episodes almost as soon as we arrived and so the first minutes of our visit were spent frantically looking for a suction machine to clear her airway.

We were accustomed to doctors whisking us in and out of their office in warp speed, rushing to get in the required number of patients to process as many patients as possible. Think total opposite. Dr. Zitelli spent almost three hours with us in that first visit. The bill, not the co-pay but the bill, was $25.00. His salary was paid by the University of Pittsburgh where he was a professor.

At this point, we had been nervously awaiting the report from her EMG for weeks. Within minutes of our being with Dr. Zitelli, the specialist who had done the test was in his office explaining to him and to us the results of the test. I am not sure what that doctor was doing at the time he got Dr. Z's call but...

Such was the respect of most everyone in the hospital for Dr. Z that they would drop what they were doing to do his bidding. I don't know when we discovered it, but at some point someone told us that Dr. Zitelli has written the definitive work on pediatric diagnostics in the world. Just this past fall, I was visiting with a young family whose daughter was being treated at Children's for cancer and had the opportunity to talk to their doctor. I dropped Dr. Zitelli's name to see what kind of response I would get and she mentioned that, a few months prior, she had been, at a medical conference in the Czech Republic and had seen there in a doctor's office Dr. Zitelli's book published in the Czech language. The man is a legend.

Incredibly, you would never know it by his demeanor or by the way he treated anyone. I have met doctors who treated patients well but were jerks to their own staff and vice versa. This guy is the real deal, kind and considerate to everyone I ever saw him interact with.

Remarkably, he always had time for us. Several times through the years, we had long periods of standing or sitting at Beth's bedside waiting to see if this was the moment the Lord would take her home. These were dark, anxious periods and Merry and I would long for Dr. Zitelli's rounds knowing that he would give us the time we needed.

We were forever asking him how long he thought she would live. If the folks at Mercy had said six months, what was his best guess? In this he proved his humanity as again and again she outlived his and everyone's predictions. The last time we asked him that question was more than fourteen years ago at a time when Beth was in intensive care for 24 straight days, a time when we made official the DNR order that is still in place. At that time, he said he couldn't imagine her living past twenty-four. The summer of 2016 she turned thirty.

Of course, we talked about more than Beth's condition. He got to know all of our girls well through their many visits and, though we met them less often, we learned much about his family. We began to feel like friends with this special man and at one point asked him if he would ever consider visiting us in our home, more than an hour from his home in Pittsburgh. Unbelievably he said, "Yes," and shortly he was spending an afternoon with us in Jefferson.

His wife, Ann, directed plays for sixth graders in their local Catholic school. Anyone who has experience with high school productions will know how difficult it is to pull off a quality show. This dear lady with the help of a tremendous support cast of parents and teachers, year after year after year, put together amazing productions. Oh, yeah, they only did Shakespeare. Sixth graders doing Shakespeare? Hard to believe? But they did it and did it well. And the entire Dorean clan was there to watch each year for probably at least six years running.

One lesson that Dr. Zitelli taught us early on is the importance of standing up for what you think is right. That sounds almost trite writing it and it is, of course, one of those things that we all are taught from childhood. But here's what I mean.

In the world of modern medicine, everyone is a professional and, therefore, everyone thinks that he/she knows what is best for your child. But the truth is that as the parent of a special needs kid like Beth, though we had none of the training of the professionals, we knew her and what she needed in many ways better than anyone else. The "I am the expert here" attitude of some folks, and even the established protocol of the hospital, can intimidate less secure folks like us into silence. Let me offer a couple of for-instances.

Because Children's is a teaching facility, Beth often received care from student nurses, usually overly solicitous and entirely pleasant. On one occasion, she was blessed with a young nurse who was administering her first shot. She had practiced on oranges, but had never stuck a live person. She was surrounded by the RN from the floor and her own nursing instructor as well as two or more Doreans. And she was scared, literally shaking, her hand twitching in hesitation over Beth's arm. After waiting for some time as the student got up her nerve, the instructor finally let out an exasperated, "Oh for God's sake, just stick her." And the poor girl punched that needle in Beth's arm with the force of an Ali uppercut. Everyone in the room let out a gasp and, of course, Beth wailed. When we told Basil of the incident he made it clear that we had every right to ask that no shots be administered by students.

And he even empowered me at one point to stand up to the head resident on a floor. As I mentioned, because of her lack of muscles, her veins and arteries are difficult to find so that she has always been a difficult stick for those drawing blood or setting an IV. None of that made any difference in the hospital's protocol.

According to that protocol the nurse assigned to Bethany got the first assignment of sticking her for an IV. Because these folks were daily the frontline for such procedures they were occasionally successful, usually after several attempts and a lot of tears and nasty words from Beth. From there it most often got worse.

Next in line was the charge nurse for the floor who with, years of experience, was deemed a more likely candidate for success. Our experience was that these folks most often had been removed by administrative responsibilities from the daily routine of shots and IVs and were therefore rarely successful when called upon. But protocol required their involvement.

Less successful still, but higher up the chain, were the residents, folks who had finished the mandatory four years of med school and were now working the floor to gain experience before setting out to their own practices. These doctors were gifted, compassionate and most always willing to talk, but frankly lacked the expertise acquired by day in and day out work in the trenches. I am not sure I can ever remember a resident performing a successful stick on Beth.

Fourth in line was the chief resident, the head guru of the floor, the "buck stops here" guy or gal in charge of everything that went on. They were always good, very good at what they did. Unfortunately inserting an IV line was not one of the things they did regularly.

But hospital protocol required that the nurse stick Beth two or three times before handing her off to the charge nurse who would stick her two or three times before handing her off to the resident who would stick her two or three times before handing her off to the chief resident who would stick her two or three times. And when all else failed, they would call in an anesthesiologist who stuck people every day all day and who rarely missed even once.

Well, on one hospital admission we groaned when Dr. Z mentioned that still another IV would be ordered and I complained about the eight to twelve sticks that meant Beth would once again endure. He said that if we wanted to we could ask that the protocol be put aside and an anesthesiologist brought in from the start. Unfortunately, he was leaving at the end of a long day and did not write that order before he left.

We got to the floor and Beth's nurse made moves to stick her for an IV. I asked for the anesthesiologist. She went for the charge nurse who went for the resident who went for the chief resident. He was pretty cocky, was sure that he could get the IV in and felt no need to call for the pro.

"Sir, there is really no need for us to trouble the anesthesiologist. I can do this."

"I would rather you didn't. Let's just get the pro now."

After five minutes of discussion, he said, "I'll tell you what. I will make one try. If I can't get it, we will get the pros."

Reluctantly I agreed. He stuck her and missed. I don't know how many IVs you have seen inserted, but these folks have a way, where when they miss, they keep prodding around with the needle inside you for a long time while they are trying to hit that moving vein. It is torture. He did that and failed again and again, finally withdrawing the needle and saying, "I'll get it this time for sure."

"No, you won't. Because there will not be a next time. We had an agreement and I expect you to honor that agreement."

He did. I felt like I had won a world war. My point in all of that is what we are so slow to learn about so much of life. In a world of experts, intimately knowing and caring for a

person is its own form of expertise that we dare not discount.
Dr. Zitelli helped us see that and empowered us to live it out
in making sure others provided the best care of Beth possible.

It has now been almost fourteen years since we have seen
Dr. Zitelli professionally, a sign of the remarkably good
health that Bethany has maintained. But almost never do we
make a trip to Children's that we do not stop by his office to

pay him a visit. Often he is on rounds, or even out of the country on some medical education event, and we visit with his delightful and incredibly capable nurse, Vicki. They remain family who have been God's ministering angels to us for more than a quarter of a century.

***

So influential did Dr. Z become in our lives so quickly that within a few months of our first meeting with him, he had persuaded us to complete a full set of updated vaccinations for all the girls.

CHAPTER FOUR

Starting Some Routines Fall 1986

BECAUSE OF THAT four hour rotation that I spoke of, sleep became one of the most treasured happenings of our days. We became resentful of each other on occasion when we felt like the other had not taken fullest advantage of the night's rest rotation. If one of us stayed up reading or watching TV when we should have been sleeping, and complained the next morning about being tired, no slack was given.

To this day, Merry and I almost never sleep together because we take turns sleeping with Beth. Gone is the fear that she might die at any moment that dominated our lives in those early months. But her lack of mobility still limits her ability to reposition herself or roll herself over the way that the rest of us do pretty much unconsciously. So she awakens anywhere from three or four times on a good night to a dozen or more times on a bad night wanting to be rolled over.

Sleeping beside her enables us to do that in a matter of a few seconds. But waking up is required. Those nights when it is our turn to sleep without being interrupted are like precious jewels to each of us. Almost every morning that I awaken when it has not been my night with Beth, and I rise feeling refreshed and eager for the new day, I wonder to myself how very different these last thirty years might have been if I could have lived them without near constant sleep deprivation. And I long to be able to help others to see what a most often unrecognized but incredible blessing sleep is.

Merry says this lack of sleep has opened her eyes to the many other people who also experience it: parents of young children, older folks who have to get up to go to the bathroom, caregivers for the sick, people who are over-stimulated or worried and many more.

In those first weeks at home, some medical or social service professional helped us get set up with a visiting nurse program. What ensued was itself something of a nightmare. These well meaning professionals would show up at 11:00 P.M., most often without a clue of what they were getting in to. So most often Merry would stay up for a half hour to an hour getting them acclimated to the routine of Beth's care and showing them where various supplies were located.

She would come to bed wound up from the responsibility of training and often unable to get to sleep right away. Once again we were both focused on maximizing our use of this precious break time, which often left us too keyed up to sleep.

You need to know that we have lived for the last thirty years in a very pleasant church parsonage that was perfectly sized for the family of four we were when we first arrived and pretty tiny for a family of six. It was especially small in those days when a "medical clinic" being run by an "intruder" was being conducted on the first floor. Beth slept in a crib in either our living room or dining room. The whole first floor is fairly open, being built around a central staircase.

All of which is to say that there really was no place to go to read a good book or to sip a cup of tea, even to wind down and chill out, so as to be able to sleep. Both of us could pretty much sleep standing up, we were so tired much of the time. But, of course, when you "have" to sleep, when your insurance company's dollars are making it possible for you to sleep, sometimes it is too much.

Then there were Merry's motherly instincts that on several occasions rightly sensed that that night's nurse was not going to work out. For instance, one night we woke up to the smell of cigarette smoke. We raced down stairs to find the nurse puffing away on what was obviously not her first cigarette, just a few feet from our baby with an oxygen mask on. She seemed pretty bent out of shape when we told her that was not acceptable. When we came down the next night to find her smoking half in and half outside of our kitchen door, we asked her to leave. Now that was more than a quarter of a century ago, long before the world became sensitized to the plight of non-smokers and it was freezing cold outside but really...

One very dear friend, who knew of our plight with several nurses who did not work out, volunteered to do one night a week for us. She was awesome, but refused to sleep at all out of concern for Beth, which left us plagued with guilt that we had cost her a full night's sleep.

***

Amidst the sometimes big crises of caring for Beth, there were some incredibly delightful moments as well. Merry's journal notes exciting progress like noticing her fingers move a little, her right foot moving just a bit. (This in a family that would not too many years later celebrate our eldest becoming a Division 3 All American in the 800 meter run. Sometimes the contrasts in what we celebrated as success were a bit overwhelming.)

A young physical therapist, Jeff Swartz (whose own boys would grow up to be Harvard trained doctors working with Dr. Paul Farmer, of <u>Mountains Beyond Mountains</u> fame) came to our house from the first days after our discharge from Mercy to do some stretching that it was hoped would help Beth grow in flexibility and strength. He quickly became a family favorite. In fact, he continued to visit Beth and all of us on a volunteer basis long after funding for the therapy was canceled by insurance. His giving spirit is a demonstration of God's provision that we have seen repeated through a myriad of other folks' generosity to us.

We have spent most of our married lives trying to live as simply as possible, so used furniture was all we ever knew. Shortly after Beth's birth, we bought a new rocking chair that we all used to cuddle with Beth in those moments in between feedings and poundings and diaper changings. It remains my favorite piece of furniture in the house, though now I curl up with a good book instead of with a sickly baby.

The journal notes a visit to Dr. Stacher in the days back in Jefferson, and the fact that he commented on our Bethany's bright eyes, still among her most attractive features. Dr. Stacher also made mention that the nurses at Greene County Memorial wanted to see Beth again. Not only did we visit but, in the next year, I would perform a wedding for one of them, an event we all attended with tremendous delight.

Almost two months after Beth was born, our church family had a prayer service that focused on her healing, a service put together by our area minister. We prayed as a congregation as we had prayed as a family that this precious baby would be touched by a miracle from God and healed in a way that the medical community on which all of us so rely had not yet brought about. No miracle happened that night, at least not the miracle for which we longed. We were not defeated by the apparently unanswered prayer, but we were certainly challenged anew to make sense of all that was going on in her life and ours, to understand with new eyes what it meant to be in the will of God. The tension of relying utterly on God, while at the same time making several trips to a variety of doctors almost every week, pulled at the simple faith formulas we had lived with for so long. The task of keeping our eyes on the Great Healer and trusting Him for our kid's wellbeing was as challenging as it was important.

So much of those early days were filled with encouraging reports that were followed closely by discouraging reports that were followed by another stay in the hospital. One such visit went over Hannah's fourth birthday so Merry and I took turns at home and in the hospital, doing our best to provide some degree of normalcy for our kids. Thirty years later, we still function best when life has a degree of normalcy, though decades ago we had to redefine a new normal.

I am not sure that I can ever remember any of the other three girls complaining because they had to give up something because of the care that Beth required. I am sure it is not true, but they never seemed to be embarrassed about having a sister with all of Beth's problems. In fact, still to this day they do their very best to touch base with her almost every day, though they are now all three at some distance from us, in Colorado, D.C. and Oklahoma. In the early days, they would each make sure they got a turn every day to hold Beth for at least a few minutes.

Merry's journal entry for September 20, 1986, a little more than two months after Beth was born, mentions a visit from a friend in the church family commenting that Bethany has already changed people's lives. That reality is still so incredibly apparent almost every day. People, young and old alike, have been significantly impacted by her life. One couple who was among the most active members in our church for years until they had a falling out with the pastor (that would be me) called or received a call from Beth every day, most often several times a day. Until the wife's death some time ago, years after leaving the church, they talked with her several times a week. And they weep anytime they talk about the difference that she has made in their lives, mentioning how, when they would be fighting between themselves, and Beth would call, their differences would evaporate in the course of talking with her.

***

Even as we are editing this in December 2016, our good friend and Beth's phone buddy, Dave Calvario (Executive Director of the County of Greene Redevelopment Authority) e-mailed us asking, "Is something wrong with Beth? She hasn't called in a few days."

***

By the middle of October, Bethany was back in Greene County Memorial. More aspiration pneumonia, high fevers, difficulty breathing. Dr. Stacher came in and straightforwardly told us to prepare ourselves because Bethany was going to die, if not that night, sometime in the very near future. Two of our closest friends were in the room when he said that and they accompanied us when, a few minutes later we walked her out of the hospital. We were still new to the medical world and had no idea of the problems we created for others in taking that walk. I figured that if she was going to die, Beth deserved one more look at the night sky. The stars were brilliant that night and the cold night air made breathing easier. As we carried her back to her room some time later, she was sleeping peacefully for the first time in days.

Dr. Stacher was furious with the nursing staff because he had returned and found us gone and they did not know where we were. We felt bad for getting them in trouble, but till the day I die I am sure that I will be glad that we did it.

Back inside, we both collapsed from exhaustion and fell asleep in chairs in Beth's room. Our good friend, Gloria Bishop held Beth for those hours when we feared for her life but just could not stay awake. Gloria and her daughters continued to pray for Bethany for many years. Like so many who have blessed us in small and large ways, they will never know our gratitude for their loving care for all of us.

That hospitalization included for the first time, at least that it was officially noted, that her lung collapsed. Mucous plugs from her inability to breathe deeply and clear the lungs became a constant worry. We began, around this time, lying her in a downward position and soon all of her percussion therapy would be done with her head sloped downwards to make drainage of the lungs easier. Because it also made

vomiting easier we had to make sure we did her feedings after
the therapy.

***

One thing that I noticed early on in our life with Bethany
was how people whom we had known for years, when they
became aware of her/our struggles, opened up about their
own. Because we were living under the doctor's assessment
that Beth would not be long for this world, many folks who
had lost children of their own but had not talked with anyone
about it for years, suddenly opened up to us. That was a
tremendous blessing to me as their pastor, as it allowed me
to love them and pray for them in ways I had never realized
they needed.

One family, whose own son suffered with Cystic Fibrosis
and had a lot of the same issues that Beth did with mucous
plugs and collapsed lungs and the necessity of percussion
therapy, opened up to us in a remarkable fashion. Over the
years we had the privilege of loving on their son in some fun
ways and got him involved in the worship life of the church
playing guitar in a way I think none of us ever dreamed might
happen.

***

Throughout these early months, of course, the routines of
family life went on, whether we had the energy to cope with
them or not. Merry's journal notes things like one daughter
having worms and another having a wart burned off and still
another getting her ears pierced for the first time, the family
learning a new song that we all sang and played together at
worship and Habitat house dedications, planning to be a part
of a friend's wedding, traveling to conferences. Friends and

family, many of them now long gone, visited and babysat and brought food to help us maintain some measure of normalcy, to allow us to spend some time with the other kids and as a couple. Never was the notion that "It takes a village to raise a child" more in evidence.

***

Through all of the stress and strain and nights with very little sleep, my brave and determined wife continued to pump breast milk.

***

In another sign of God's remarkable goodness to us through His people, several other ladies in the community pumped breast milk for Beth that we would freeze and give to her when Merry's supply ran low.

In periods when doctors' visits slowed a bit, we would take Beth at least once a week to the Post Office where we would weigh her on their scales. The postmistress was a dear saint of the church family and, for quite a while, Beth was small enough to fit comfortably on their package scale. Because of all her issues with reflux and frequent refluxing, NG tube feedings and the like, charting her weight gains and losses was one of the most accurate ways we had of tracking her progress to see how well she was thriving.

***

That first Christmas Merry wrote me a poem that leaves me teary-eyed every time I read it.

To Daddy From Bethany

Daddy, I want to thank you
For loving me like you do;
For running my hand along your beard
And listening to me coo.

Your tender hands have touched me
From the moment of my birth
Your love has kept me covered,
It's the sweetest thing on earth.

If you think that I've forgotten
How you drove up to the city
And always gave encouragement
Instead of only pity,

You'd be wrong, 'cause I remember,
I have stored up every song.
Every smile, every story,
Every kiss the whole year long.

The times when I'm alone
Or my trouble doesn't cease,
I think of your good caring
And I rest in perfect peace.

I haven't much to give you
Just a smile and a coo
But I'll try my very hardest
To grow big and strong like you.

You remind me of Our Father
Whose little child I am
I thank Him for the blessing
That I'm also Daddy's lamb.

Beth's Grandma Posey wrote a story of those first months with her. She and Grandpa lived at the eastern end of Pennsylvania but were back and forth a lot in those early days with Beth. I think the thing that stood out most to her was Bethany's determination to keep on fighting. She credits that night outside the hospital under the stars for Beth's resolve. All of us give the glory to God but, the kid has been remarkable in her perseverance. So many times we have thought she was dying, so many times she could have just given up, but each time she has fought back. It is nothing short of amazing.

Mom Posey remembers something I had forgotten until I recently reread her story. Because Beth could not make a sound in the early days, her means of communicating her excitement in seeing us or having us sing to her was to flail her little arms around, she would almost flap them like a bird, arms bent at the elbows. And from somewhere she learned to stick her tongue out, not in any sense as a normal kid does as a kind of "in your face" gesture. For Beth her tongue, like her flapping arms, was a means of expressing her joy and delight and often brought us to tears.

Today, when she gets excited, that tongue is still her means of communicating, but now it runs on in endless questions. Just the other night I let her call a family friend who she has a "Beth crush" on. He is a freshman in college, away at school, quite firmly committed to a beautiful young woman. And Beth gets none of that. She just talks about him and others like him (there is quite a list) and seems to get endless pleasure in just thinking about him. When she got the chance to talk to him, she just started with a seemingly endless list of questions. "How's your dad? How's your mom? What are you doing right now? What time did you get up this morning? What are you doing tonight?" Not one question got answered before she went on to the next. And the poor kid was left trying to get an answer in somehow, but that tongue just wagged on and on unable to stop to listen. God bless him and the other men, young and old, who are her special favorites and who get assaulted by her loving banter from time to time. And God bless the women, young and old, who have learned not to take offense when she zooms by them in her wheelchair to speak to and get a hug from the nearest available man.

Looking back over the journal I find myself somewhat astounded that we kept it together at all. There are constantly, certainly weekly, notes about fevers that came on suddenly, regular issues with feedings and always, always issues of sleep. We began more experimentation with different kinds of formulas to see if that might help digestive issues, various drugs to help with reflux and mucous secretions. Each new one had its initial benefits, but all of them in the end had their issues.

***

It is amazing to see how incredibly far she has come. Today, at age thirty, Beth gets a shot of Lovenox to prevent blood clots. And we give her some Tylenol at night to try to help her sleep (or more accurately to ease some of her pain so that she can sleep better.) But that's it. For the last thirteen years or more she has been healthier, at least from the perspective of getting routine colds and flu, than either Merry or I. In those first months, having her healthy for a day or a two at a time was a miracle.

***

And her fighting to breathe and swallow and digest food did nothing to prevent her from the regular childhood diseases like chicken pox. Oh, yeah, sister Hannah got them at school and about a week later Beth had them as well. Soon we were swaddling her to prevent her scratching the pox.

***

CHAPTER FIVE

First Surgeries Spring 1986

A FTER SEVERAL DISASTROUS encounters, by January 1987 we had two visiting nurses whom we really liked and who were great to work with. They would most often come at night to allow us to sleep. Though by the time they came and we debriefed the day with them, and then got up before they were scheduled to leave to hear how the night had gone, we were eternally grateful to be able to catch a few more winks than if we had been without them.

And then there was the constant flow of equipment and the ever-present issue of where to keep it all. And for that matter, where to keep Beth. We had a child-sized hospital bed that we could crank the head and foot up and down on so as to make the every four hour "pounding" work more efficiently. This allowed Beth to sleep through the night in a downward position for optimal draining of mucous from her lungs. That bed started out staying in the living room, and then got shifted to the dining room, as we tried to keep her in the center of our lives and allow for the rest of the household to sleep when the round-the-clock therapy and feeding went on throughout the night. Feeding pumps, suction machines, various oxygen apparatuses, equipment to help her sit and then later to stand, all had to find a place in our increasingly crowded house. Today much of that equipment is gone, as are Beth's three sisters. A room got added on just for her, and we still feel crowded at times.

***

March of 1987 saw two significant developments on the medical front. While Beth's sisters were busy spending some special nights with friends and prepping for ballet recitals, all of us were gearing up for her first real surgery. Remarkably we all fit in a five day trip to Chicago where all four girls were in a wedding for two of our closest friends, Jon and Maribeth Coote. Friends and family made each of the other three girls' dresses, and Merry somehow found time and energy to create the matching one for Beth. Merry's mom came out and flew with Merry and Bethany to Chicago while I drove out with some friends in their Chevy Astro minivan. Shockingly, everything went smoothly, at least relatively speaking. We made it to the Aquarium and the Science and Industry Museum and had a wonderful time, though Merry and Beth had to pull back and rest when Beth seemed to be crashing.

When we returned from Chicago, we started prepping for the surgery, the placement of a stomach tube to replace the nose tube with which we had been feeding her since day one. It was a day that would change our lives in many ways.

Because we had had Beth at Mercy for the first six weeks or so, some of her doctors from that hospital were still among those we had contact with. In this case that meant that we were seeing a gastroenterologist, Dr. Chandra, who was based at Mercy. But he was not a surgeon so was handing that off to a Dr. Weiner at Children's who everyone assured us was top of the line. Dr. Chandra was a great people person, made us feel comfortable and assured us that the placement of a g-tube was a very simple procedure and that it would make life infinitely easier.

Keep in mind that Beth lived with an NG-tube for about six months, which meant that she went around with a tube hanging from her nose wherever she went. On Sundays we would often remove it to give her and, I suppose, ourselves, some sense of dignity with the crowd of church folks. Anytime we removed it, we had to reinsert it, which involves gagging her, sticking the tube down her throat. It was never pleasant, though we and she got used to it, as much as you can get used to something like that.

Beth had issues with another collapsed lung the day before the surgery so we had to be extremely aggressive with PT so that the surgery, though simple, could go ahead. The night before surgery the anesthesiologist came in to do his routine of explaining this is what to expect and this is what could go wrong. We have now been through numerous surgeries with Beth, but this was our first with anyone in the family. And while I have now been through it dozens of times in pre-op with parishioners, I had never heard the protocol speech before. I mean we thought we were doing a simple half hour procedure and this guy left us thinking that we could face our kid never coming back from the operating table. We were devastated. If you are saying, "naive," you would be right. But the list of all the things that could go wrong was overwhelming.

We called Dr. Chandra to make sure that, in light of all that could go wrong, he still felt it was worth proceeding. He assured us that they had to tell everyone what could go wrong to prevent lawsuits. His assurances allayed our fears a bit.

The next morning we were up early and met, for the first time, Dr. Weiner, whose people skills were among the worst I have ever encountered. He told us that we should be doing a much more complicated surgery that involved a fundoplication, which involves surgically wrapping the top of the stomach around the bottom of the esophagus and stitching it in place, to reinforce the closing function at the top of the stomach. This would prevent the kind of reflux issues that had plagued Beth with so many aspiration pneumonias. He treated us like fools for not doing the more involved surgery and predicted that we would be back soon to have it done. He was right on all counts, but so brutal that he left us filled with guilt and fear and uncertainty, not what you are looking for when you are turning your kid over to her first surgeon. Dr. Chandra was more of a minimalist and felt that given Beth's fragile state, less was more and so had not pushed us at all to think about the more serious surgery.

The day of the surgery all went well. Beth did great. She was on Pedialyte the first day and was taking breast milk and formula by the second day. Dr. Weiner showed up the second day and said that her lung had never fully re-inflated and would likely someday have to be removed. The guy was good.

The left lung would last about another fourteen years, but was a constant source of infection producing endless pneumonias. When it was finally removed (the operation was put off so long because no one thought Beth could survive the surgery), it was performed by a cardio-thorasic surgeon who had both the medical and the people skills that we needed. Her health saw a complete turnaround from that moment on. But that is a story for later.

As we were preparing to leave the hospital about five days after the surgery (for most folks a tube placement is a same day surgery but Beth's lung issues kept us a lot longer), Dr. Weiner came in and explained that we would need to come to the hospital every few months to have the tube changed. He was no sooner out of the room, than Sally Foster, a remarkably gifted woman who was assigned the responsibility of helping with folks' transition from hospital to home, took us aside and basically said, "There ain't no way." She explained and demonstrated how simple tube placement was, once the initial surgery had been performed, and that it was nonsensical to have us drive more than an hour one way to have someone else take five minutes to do what we could easily do for ourselves at home. So we, mostly Merry, have been changing tubes ever since. After a few years, we switched to a McKee button, a nifty device to which you attach a feeding tube but which reduces the ugly hassle of having a foot long blue tube tucked under your shirt.

As it turned out, we were back at Children's much sooner than expected, with a visit to Greene County Memorial in between. It had become apparent within a three week period that Dr. Weiner had been right and that the fundoplication was necessary. That marked the end of our dealings with anyone from Mercy and we moved forward more and more under Dr. Zitelli's care. Beth had the fundo, all went well and it made an enormous difference for her. For several months afterwards, Beth was on a continuous feeding pump for her nutritional intake. That worked well, though it tended to limit her mobility (and ours) a bit. We kept that up until during a visit with Dr. Weiner he told us to cut off night feedings, so as to help us gain a little more of a normal life.

***

As Beth turned one year old, it was amazing how busy we all stayed. We went to about three different birthday parties for our girl, Merry took all four girls up north to vacation for five days with some friends who ran a bed and breakfast near Presque Isle where they did berry picking and hung out on the beach (Beth was in the shade most of the time.) Merry and I were both volunteering significant numbers of hours with Habitat for Humanity, as were the three older girls, who would often go off with me for a Saturday work day.

***

This was the time that we began to deal with two other aspects of Beth's health. The muscle weakness had been evident in her eyes pretty much since birth. Her one eye drifted, so that sometimes it was working well and other times it looked crossed and other times it was looking outwards. This was one of those situations where Dr. Zitelli's ability to direct us to the right professional was invaluable. We had been to an eye doctor who wanted to give her glasses. Knowing our girl better than he, we realized she would never have kept them on. Basil referred us to Dr. Biglan. I have often described him as the Mr. Rogers of optometrists. He very much had Fred Rogers' gentle, quiet personality, yet was, like his alter ego, every bit the professional you wanted to have dealing with your kid. He did surgery on Beth's eyes in September of 1987 when she was thirteen months old and thoroughly delighted us with the news the next day that everything looked "perfect." She now uses one eye for distance and one for close-up, more or less, so her eyes are not always focused together. They are way better than they used to be, but not perfect.

Perfect and Beth are not words that one puts in the same sentence very often. She has oh so many things "wrong" with her. And yet, maybe because she has so many things "wrong"

with her, in many ways she is much of the time closer to heaven or heaven-likeness than the rest of us. Oh, for sure, she has a nasty tongue that spits out words like "I hate you" or "You're fat and ugly," when she gets upset about getting her shot or having someone do anything to her wheelchair or just not getting her way. And yet she is willing to accept the unacceptable and love the unlovable better than just about anyone I know.

***

That summer of '87 was a hot one. Merry and I had spent seven summers in southwest Georgia in a Christian community, Koinonia Partners, that was committed to living simply and would have looked at air-conditioning as a wild indulgent luxury. But when occasionally that summer we were in places that had air-conditioning, we noticed what a difference it made in the ease with which Beth could breathe.

When we mentioned this casually to some friends in the church, the next thing we knew the Ladies' Christian Circle of the church was volunteering to put whole house air-conditioning in the parsonage in the hope that it would make life easier for our girl. And it undoubtedly has been a lifesaver, dramatically easing her breathing when things get hot and humid. Just another example of the incredible love and care our church family has always shared with us.

***

CHAPTER SIX

Serving Others Summer & Fall 1987

I HAVE MENTIONED PREVIOUSLY how Beth's life ministered to other folks even as so many ministered to her and all of us. Nowhere, I think, was that more obvious than in her relationship with my Mom, Jeanne Rich. My dad, Bennett Rich, scholar, university professor, and college president died in 1984, two and a half years before Bethany was born. I have often thought that that was God's mercy. My dad was a remarkable man, gentle, humble, serving. He was definitely of the generation that did not wear their emotions on their sleeves. I only saw my dad cry once and that was in explaining to us how one of his colleagues at Rutgers, a young man, had cancer and was going to die.

I think Dad would have had a very difficult time watching Beth go through all that she has endured and watching her family walk those early years with her.

My mom, by contrast, was upbeat and joyful, outgoing and caring. She and my dad were twenty-nine and thirty-nine respectively when they met and loved each other with one of those never-ending loves. My mom was a different woman after Dad died. His passing robbed her not only of a soulmate but the object of her love.

An operation to remove a tumor in her brain years later further changed her personality. My brother, who married a year later than us, and who lived at a distance, has commented how his kids only knew that grumpier, almost mean

Grandma. I get that, because it seems like when my dad died a lot of the joy wilted inside my mom.

But Beth was a saving grace in my mom's life. Merry's mom and dad had made several trips clear across the state in the early months and had moved in to provide day to day care for all of us for a week or more at a time. My mom never moved in or ever offered that kind of day by day, hour by

hour care. But Merry's journals are full of references like: Grandma came and watched Beth while we went food shopping; Grandma took the girls to ballet lessons; we had dinner at Grandma's; we went out to dinner at Pizza Hut with Grandma. Week after week, month after month, year after year, these times with Grandma are noted.

My mom learned to feed Beth and change her and do percussion therapy. She had to. But I remember her, well into her seventies, getting down on the floor where we would often put Beth to encourage her to roll around. The two of them would laugh (well Beth would be flailing her arms and wagging that tongue) and talk (again always one-sided). The other girls to be sure had a good relationship with their grandma, but I think in a special way my mom poured herself into Beth. And that channel for her love gave her a reason to keep going. I don't want to make too much of that. Mom was a devout Christian who loved the Lord and for whom church and her various women's Bible studies were extremely important. But she needed a place to let her love shine and, I think, Beth was that outlet, for which we are very grateful indeed.

***

At about fourteen months Bethany began to utter her first intelligible sounds. We worked hard to get her to say, "mama" and "dada." Once she got going with those, soon to follow were "lala" for Emily, "caca" for Carrie and "nana" for Hannah. Any parent can relate to the incredible delight in hearing your kid speak your name. Ours was magnified simply because we were not certain in the early days that she would ever make a sound.

***

As she grew more stable, I began a practice that continues still to this day of taking Beth with me on pastoral calls. Initially, I did it because Merry needed a break. I should have done it more. I think it took me about twenty years to realize the stress and emotional hardship that caring day in and day out for Beth has taken on my wife. Not that I have been an absentee dad. I have worked really hard to take an active part of all of my kids' lives. In thirty-five years as pastor I have rarely worked less than fifty and often more than seventy hours a week. But most of the time I have been able to schedule that around what's going on in the family's life or to take my kids with me whenever and wherever I could.

And that has been even more true in Beth's life. I have tried to be the dad she has needed, the husband my wife has needed me to be. But I had a lot of distractions from the daily emotional burden of caring for Beth. Often those distractions were burdens of a different sort, but caring for a parishioner in time of need is very different than doing one more feeding, changing one more diaper, watching her growing up and not becoming the scholar/athlete you had come to expect and be proud of in your other three.

So to give Merry a chance to play the piano with Peggy Parker or to exercise or to take a nap or do something special with one of the other girls, I would load Beth up and take her to visit shut-ins. We were an older church in those days so I used to do a lot of that. And while Beth's presence then and still today will make the visit a different kind of experience than if it were just me, I think that most would regard a visit with her a real blessing.

When her own health was fragile, I would leave her at home when I was doing hospital visits, but today she loves nothing more than traveling with me to a hospital to visit someone she knows. Her favorite visits are to newborns and their moms. Don't get in her way when she is on her way to see a baby. She zooms through the halls in her power chair at breakneck speeds. It is such a joy to see her thrill at visiting God's latest gift.

Merry has been present at the birth of eight of our nine grandchildren (as well as probably a dozen other births). I guess Beth comes by her passion for babies naturally. Beth and I don't get to be in on that part of things, but we are not far behind. It is one of her "I am talking about nothing else for two weeks" subjects that can drive me mad: where she and I are going to be when the baby is born and how we're going to get to the hospital when we get the call.

It started with the birth of our first two grandsons, Asa and Phin John, who were born at McGee Women's Hospital in Pittsburgh when Matt and Emily were living there while he was doing his residency at UPMC. Beth and I got to come up when Mom got the call that things were starting to happen and we slept in their house while the other three went to the hospital. They made the mistake of calling in the wee small hours to tell us that Asa was born because Beth would not think about going back to sleep but had to get there "Now Dad" to help take care of him.

With Phin John, we did the same thing except this time we were entrusted with Asa's care and had to drag him along with us. There was no stopping Aunt Beth. Her fascination and determination have only intensified with each passing birth. Hannah and Craig's first, also born at McGee while Craig also was doing a residency at UPMC, has been the most intense. Beth had to share those earliest hours after birth with Craig's family and that seems to only have ratcheted up her passion for little Clara. "When are we going to see Clara, Dad? Can we Facetime with Clara, Dad? I need to help Hannah take care of Clara, Dad."

***

So a word about feedings is in order. When after nine months or so, Merry decided to stop pumping, we began the search for alternatives.

We went through a wide variety of formulas and were never sure which ones were creating increased secretions because she possibly had an allergy to them. By about fifteen months we had made the switch to a blenderized diet of regular foods. We worried for a while that perhaps she had

an allergy to milk but pressed on.

Pretty much that has meant, for thirty years now, my good wife has once every three or four days been taking fruits, vegetables, yogurt, oats, olive oil, and some supplements like vitamins and calcium, putting them through some sort of blender/food processor and creating Beth's food. Most of the time we stretch that batch of food by adding a can or two of formula.

I am certain that one of the reasons Bethany has done as well as she has is precisely because she "eats" so well. No sugar, no junk food of any kind enters that kid's system. Actually, we have the last few years worked to thin her food by adding more water so that she doesn't get too heavy. We are increasingly aware of our own limitations in lifting her as we get older. And, of course, additional weight puts more strain on her whole system that is not good for her. But it is a very different life in trying to keep weight off of her than keeping it off the rest of us. As one who is forever exercising an hour a day to keep my weight under control, there is a part of me that wishes I could just add a little water to my system and lose weight.

We have gone through a lot of blenders through the years, each one of them increasingly of better quality and higher priced. In the early days we were still fixated on doing things simply and cheaply. But as the years have passed, it has increasingly become about durability and convenience. A few years back our eldest daughter, Emily, bought us a really nice and very expensive processor that has been a real blessing. I used to do some of the work of making Beth's food but do it almost never today, except on those rare occasions when Merry gets a few days to visit her mom or some such travel option.

For the sake of truth in advertising, I should mention that while Beth ingests nothing bad for her, she does love to taste foods which she has learned to then spit out rather than trying to swallow. And her tastes definitely run towards junk food. Potato chips of most any variety and French fries are her favorite, so we often buy one of those containers with twenty little bags of a variety of chips that she will open while lying on her gurney watching TV. I think it is the salt that she loves best. But it is kind of comical seeing this thirty year old lying down with barbecue chip remains smeared across her face and hands smiling with this devilish grin like she just got away with something like some little kid.

***

By November of 1987 Beth was saying, or almost saying, "My Papa." Wow! Was I the proud dad? It continues to amaze me how little things like that continue to give me great joy. Presently Beth and I are visiting a guy in the hospital and she always has me tell his wife that she is here and is going to help take care of him. (She could, of course, tell the wife that herself but needs to have it announced.)

That same month, Merry and I went to the mall to see a movie, and I stopped at one of those little middle of the aisle shops and bought Beth some fleece-lined soft leather moccasins to keep her feet warm. It is an interesting dynamic that the kid is certainly a million dollar baby in terms of the medical costs of keeping her alive, but we do very little to spoil her in any way. Hospital visits always garnered her a gazillion stuffed animals, none of which she became attached to and so quickly got passed on to others who appreciated them more. But those moccasins made it into Merry's journal, I think, because it was rare for us to splurge on Beth. I guess it was the habit/discipline we developed early on in our married life. Our eighth grandchild is wearing them now.

In that same month, we had our first official visit with Dr. Tim Ward, an orthopedic surgeon at Children's. He had actually taken a look at Beth on our first visit with Dr. Zitelli.

But this visit began what will certainly be a lifelong discussion about scoliosis. Even then, Beth's back was beginning to twist, a result of the muscle weakness that runs throughout her body. She does not have the muscle strength to keep her spine straight, so it is bending and twisting.

A couple of things are worth noting. For most of the next fifteen years, we would visit Dr. Ward every six months to check on the progress of the scoliosis. Every time we went, we got x-rays of her back and every time the results were the same: her condition is worsening. From one of our earliest visits, Dr. Ward talked about the fact that, when she stopped growing, we would insert a rod up her back that would make sitting more comfortable and would improve her lung capacity because she wouldn't be hunched over much of the time. In the meantime, Beth started getting fitted for a brace.

I was fascinated in reading Merry's journal that on this visit in November of 1987, Dr. Ward was talking about fitting her for leg braces with the hope that she might walk. I don't know whether he was trying to keep us encouraged about her future or like the rest of us still in the dark about the seriousness of her condition. But the fact is that Beth has never come close to walking. Years later we would start strapping her into a stander that enabled her to be upright for short periods of time. The goal was to help her legs bear some weight to keep them strong, less brittle. But that was almost always painful, and though we kept at it for years, and even once purchased a wheelchair that enabled her to go from a sitting to a standing position, we eventually gave up entirely.

After years and years of those every six month visits, Dr. Ward concluded that Beth would likely not survive the surgery to place a rod. So that idea got shelved and, unfortunately, our relationship with him ended as well. That came at his suggestion, as about all he could do for us was to chronicle her worsening scoliosis. He was a wonderful guy and we were kind of sorry to lose that occasional visit with him. The last x-ray we saw of her back, Beth's spine looked almost like an S. It is hard to imagine that someone can live with that severe a condition. Of course, eventually the curvature of the spine would crush the left lung and make its removal necessary. But that is a later part of the story.

***

CHAPTER SEVEN

Difficult Choices Spring Summer 1988

I HAVE WRITTEN OF how a wide variety of people opened up parts of their lives to us in ways they had never before shared with anyone when they knew of our struggles with Beth. But there was another phenomena at work all around us as well that shaped our lives profoundly. And that came in realizing that no matter how bad things got for Beth or for us as her family, there were always people who had it so much worse. Nowhere was that more evident to us than in our early days in the ICU at Children's in 1987-88.

As I remember it, the ICU was just one big open room with bed after bed of very sick children. There were private rooms that were reserved for those with contagious infections. We got in those a couple of times. But even those rooms were pretty much all glass so that you could see out and others could see in and there was a total lack of privacy.

Not that anyone cared about the lack of privacy. When you are fighting for your kid's life, and everyone in that unit was doing just that, you just didn't care if folks saw you in some embarrassing poses.

But it also meant that you could always look around and see the struggles of those around you, sometimes overhear discussions with doctors, observe medical procedures that your own child had not yet experienced.

There was one group of kids whom I will never forget as long as I live. These kids were golden in color, really, golden. Their bodies were swollen so completely that they looked like the Pillsbury Doughboy, like if you stuck them with a pin they would explode. And standing beside them would be these totally white parents. I can remember thinking for the longest time that they must have been adopted. How else would these white parents have these golden skinned babies?

How else? Liver failure. These kids were almost all desperately waiting for a liver transplant. At the time Children's was one of the leading facilities in the nation for liver transplants and these kids were waiting their turn, praying for their turn, hoping for their turn to receive a liver that quite literally would be the difference between a fairly normal existence and almost certain death.

We would be in that ICU with Beth who was more than likely fevered, usually on oxygen, fighting for every breath, uncomfortable and, more often than not, unable to sleep because of the lights that shined 24/7, most often losing weight as she often suffered from diarrhea and choking episodes. And we would be feeling like life had let us down, like God had abandoned us, like things couldn't get any worse. And then we would look up from our little curtained off area and see kids and families whose struggles made ours seem pale by comparison.

***

In the early months of 1988 with Beth at about a year and a half old and weighing about 16 pounds, it is incredible to realize that most normal days contained some medical issue. Either her tube was clogged and needed to be cleaned out or replaced or she was running a fever with diarrhea and had to go off her regular formula and be put on Pedialyte to prevent dehydration. So then we were constantly concerned about getting her enough calories so that she could thrive as best as possible. Or she was congested and needed to lie on a downward slant, or to have more percussion therapy, or to have an antibiotic administered that most often had its own side effects that we had to combat. The number of trips to Children's for checkups or procedures or to stay for a few nights was endless.

***

We became real professionals at all of the ins and outs of life at Children's. The Pop Shop, a snack place that was open longer hours than the cafeteria made one of the best milk shakes I have ever tasted. And I consider myself quite a connoisseur of milk shakes. We learned how to park reasonably cheaply and how to put in our name for one of the few rooms they made available every night for parents who were staying in the hospital but trying to get a bit more sleep than one could hope to get sleeping in one of the recliners in your kid's room.

Beth did not like us sleeping in those rooms. We would always leave the nurses instructions to wake us if she woke up and needed us for any reason. Nurses, who had been at the job a while and had a sense for how bone tired we were, sometimes were able to resist her charm or the fake cries with which she enticed the less experienced into calling us two, three, four times in the five or six hours we were trying to sleep. And every call meant a trip from the floor where the rooms were to Beth's room. Oh, the pain of waking up and then the need to try to gear back down so as to be able to try to sleep again.

These early months in 1988 were filled with one trip after another to the hospital. Beth's left lung was almost always partially collapsed, creating all sorts of issues. That meant that we were doing percussion therapy vigorously multiple times a day, keeping her in a downwards position when she was lying down and doing our best to keep her from getting exposed to anyone else's illness. On one trip to Children's, after a particularly difficult night, Merry's journal notes her crying with Dr. Zitelli and this ominous note. "Thinking it might be better if you went to heaven."

It's a thought that was never far from our minds, I suppose, though we rarely gave vent to it. Life was so very difficult for Beth, always choky with mucous running from that lung, never able to eat, so limited in her ability to move anywhere on her own, unable to communicate. Is it fair of us to make her fight through one more day, one more sickness? And then there was the toll on us, our marriage, our kids.

The very next note in the journal is this: "This is just a job, like all other hard jobs in the world, only way more meaningful." And that's it, way more meaningful. As I write this particular paragraph on a Saturday afternoon in November, 2014, I am just back from a very small, intimate wedding at the church. Merry and I were invited to go along with the wedding party to an upscale restaurant but had to decline, largely because of Beth, who just does not do well in tight spots like restaurants almost always are. It is not a big deal, but just an example of one of the thousands of ways our life is limited by her condition. So incredibly many things we might have done, places we might have visited, and yet they simply do not compare to the richness that life with her has brought us.

On that same hospital visit, in another one of our heart to hearts with Dr. Z, we discussed for the first time putting in place a DNR, an order to not resuscitate if she were to go into cardiac arrest or to apply any extreme measures to preserve her life. On this occasion we talked about it, maybe even verbally told him that those were our wishes, but never put anything in place.

***

In addition to percussion therapy and the downward positioning, another tool in our arsenal was the ever present suction machine. Suctioning had been a regular part of our life with Beth from the beginning and would continue so for more than a decade.

That said, we all hated it and always debated its efficacy. For the record, there are two kinds of suctioning which we practiced. The variety with which most folks are familiar from watching it happen to someone in the hospital is sticking a suction catheter in the mouth to help clear built up mucous. In most cases that is done with a suction wand that is the size of a thin toothbrush. That was never bad and though Beth didn't like it, when it was necessary, it was most often welcomed. But then there was deep suctioning which we performed off and on for years. Here we would do percussion therapy, "pounding," to loosen the mucous building up on the walls of her lungs and then insert a much thinner catheter up her nose and down past her gag reflex to aid her in getting that mucous up.

Again muscle weakness prevented an effective cough that would have helped clear her. Depending on how much junk we were getting out, we would have to do that process several times every couple of hours. It sounds gruesome and was, though like every other tough thing in life, you get used to it. Sort of.

The problem was, of course, that too much suctioning had a tendency to produce more mucous itself, so there was always a thin line between not enough and too much. This became another one of those many points where we would sometimes have to stand our ground against respiratory therapists who were alternately, to our mind, too aggressive or too passive. Dr. Z. trained us to realize that we knew our kid better than anyone because we had such a history with her. So often, not always, we would be able to know what she needed better than anyone. We valued him so much because, before making any evaluation, he listened to what we thought was going on. How we have learned to value other medical professionals who do the same.

***

A note in Merry's journal from May of 1988 (written as if to Bethany) recorded my reactions to a visit with Dr. Zitelli: "Dad was depressed by his (Zitelli's) continued prognosis of a short life. He also said you are mentally retarded. Today Mom got depressed. It only lasts a day. You are too wonderful for us to care about words."

It is not like Merry and I did not live every day very much aware of both of those things: that Beth was not likely to live long and that she was, obviously, not of the same intellectual prowess as our other girls. But there was something about having someone else put the reality into words that just pulled us down. But then after a while you realize that they are really just words that don't define Beth's life or our life with her and that we just need to trust that God is in all the details and keep pressing on.

***

I am not positive, but it looks to me from our journals like June of 1988, twenty-three months after she was born, was the first month that Beth was not hospitalized. In fact, she barely went to see a doctor. What she did do was make two fairly long trips, the first one with just her mom. Merry took her to her home town of Bryn Athyn, PA, a little north of Philadelphia, to visit with her mom and dad, sisters and brothers, and their families. And about a week after they got home from that trip, we were all off again to visits friends at Jubilee Partners in Comer, GA and then on to Savannah where Beth got her first experience of the sun and the surf. Well, OK, she just lay on a towel on the beach, but what an impressive achievement. From Georgia, we all drove north for a fourth of July gathering with all of Merry's family.

***

That month also recorded a bit of a freak accident. We had taken Beth to one of my church softball games. She was lying on a blanket on the grass about forty feet from first base when the opposing team's shortstop, who had an incredible arm, threw a ball to first that just got away from him. It flew past the first baseman and hit Beth in the lip, the forehead and then went on to strike Merry. The poor guy came running over and, when he saw Beth bleeding from the lip, he burst into tears, as did Merry, and the game was halted until we were sure that she was OK.

An incident like that could be really upsetting. After all the kid has been through, you would think, or at least I did, that God could have altered the trajectory of that throw to first just a minute degree so that it missed her. But He didn't and she survived and we were infinitely a lot more careful more careful from that point on in protecting her from the occasional accident.

***

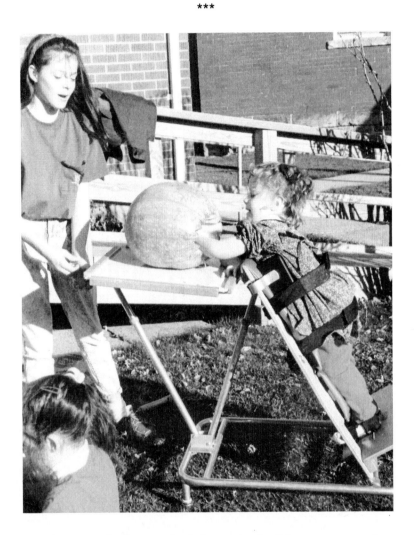

That month also marked the arrival of the prone stander. We had experimented with several different ones before biting the proverbial bullet and purchasing one. She seemed to like it, at least at first.

It became a part of her daily routine to once or twice a day spend anywhere from five minutes to more than an hour in the stander. The medical reason was strengthening her bones through weight bearing.

But I think we all, Bethany included, were fascinated by the change of perspective that it brought us all. Remember that until the stander, literally, every moment of her first two years was spent either lying flat or, more likely, on a downward incline, or sitting up in a corner chair or car chair. So we never saw her as a normal kid who stands and runs around and does other things kids do. So to suddenly see her standing there required another set of lenses to look at her life through. And for her, she was seeing the world for the first time from our perspective and not sideways.

At some point, that prone stander was replaced by a mobile stander that she could move herself in by pushing its large wheels much as if in a wheel chair. She never gained the strength to go far but we lit up when she moved herself around the house in it.

***

I am not exactly sure when we first realized it, but we noticed from early on that Beth has a special sensitivity to sound. As in, she doesn't like loud noises. Though to be clear, it is not apparent what exactly triggers her negative reaction to loudness. As mentioned earlier, she and I sing in the shower in the morning, and one of her every day phrases relates to whether Mom is still sleeping. "Mom is still sleeping so we have to sing quietly." Or what she prefers, "Mom is awake (or not here) so we can sing loud." Anyone who knows me knows that I am pretty loud, like all the time, and especially when I sing. And the more I ramp it up in the shower, the bigger the thrill for Beth.

But go to a football game, a basketball game or, God forbid, a wrestling match where there is a packed house and the crowd is raucously loud, you had better get that girl out of there quickly. I mention wrestling which, for reasons unknown to us, she has developed a near paranoia about, even though some of her most favorite men in the world are wrestlers. My best guess as to the reason for her dislike stems from my taking her when she was pretty young to a Waynesburg University wrestling match. It was a close match against an arch rival and the crowd was very loud indeed. She has never wanted to go to another and will start freaking out if there is any mention of our doing so.

But it is not just crowd noises. It can be singing or acting or anywhere that the noise is likely to push her level of comfort. She survives those occasions if there is a place that she can get away from the loudness. The Waynesburg University performing arts center where we attend two or three plays a year works fine because she can readily access the hallway away from the noise. She likes to go to high school basketball games or volleyball games, too, but don't expect to find her actually watching the game. Depending on the size of the crowd or the volume of the cheering, she is found most often cruising around the halls in her power chair chatting up one person or another too slow to avoid her.

We do our best to think through places or events that are likely to cause her problems, but it can be difficult to predict. And it can go from "Everything's fine and dandy" to a few minutes later she is in a state of complete melt down.

CHAPTER EIGHT

Making Changes 1989

SEPTEMBER OF 1988 saw Emily return to homeschooling for a year. A word needs to be said about that. For us, homeschooling was not an anti-public school crusade. We strongly believe in public education and had tasted way too much of the "religious private school" systems, which were sometimes just a code word for segregated racist academies in the South, during our years in Georgia.

Merry felt that kids should be encouraged to spend as much time with their families when they were young as possible. She felt that the whole push to socialize kids at an early age by getting them out of the home and into school was misdirected.

So when we moved to Jefferson, we kept Emily at home through the third grade. It did not make us popular, at least with some of the administrative folks in the school district, but we persisted. Carrie we sent only through the second grade and by the time Hannah made it to school, she only stayed home a year. The burden of caring for Beth at that time was just too much for Merry to carry on with teaching.

But by the time she was in eighth grade, Emily decided that she wanted to homeschool for a year, and it seemed to us a wise decision. She got more than her fair share of child care

responsibilities as part of her core curriculum. All of the girls did extremely well academically in high school and college and matured into a faith that has been central to their lives, so we have always felt like it all worked out well for them.

I mention this all only because there is a note in Merry's journal not long into that last year that we homeschooled, in mid-September, where Merry confesses: "Thinking that homeschooling may just be too much." As I have read back over the journals of these early years with Beth, I want to attach my own addendum: "All of life may just be too much."

It seems phenomenal to me reading those journals how we managed to do softball and track and cross country and volleyball and swimming and Habitat and piano and dance and friendships and quality family time and… And care for an incredibly sick child through it all. Yikes!!!

***

Maybe it is because we didn't know for so long whether Beth would ever make any verbal sounds, but all of us have always taken a very special joy in many things that come out of her mouth. That is not to say that we are particularly grateful for the string of abusive words that she can cut loose with when she gets angry. Nor does it mean that we are always enthralled when she goes on and on in her non-stop questioning or endless chatter. But she has this way of picking up on something that one of us has said and making it her own that is incredibly charming. In June of '89 she started calling me her "main man." We've no idea at all where that came from, and fortunately for the rest of the world, it didn't last too long, but I sure loved it while it lasted.

Somewhere along the line she transformed a simple word like "exactly" into "eggsactly" which is only spoken in a very slow and dramatic fashion. And at not quite two years old, she had learned to fake a snore which she would use to our riotous laughs. She's also really good at a fake yawn.

***

One of the truly amazing things about Beth is how she is aware of what's going on around her. It was true at the age of two and it is still the case. We often will turn to her to ask where something in the house is. Keep in mind that this is a young woman who spends her waking hours probably evenly split between a wheelchair and her gurney. So she has limited mobility and yet, quite seriously, she has a better sense of

where things in the house are than we do. This afternoon she asked me to get her cards (she loves to lie on her gurney and just put one card in front of the other). I looked around and couldn't see them and told her I couldn't find them. "They're on the couch, Dad." That couch was at the head of the gurney in a position she could not possibly have seen. Nor could she have personally put them there. Maybe she had seen them there when she was in her chair earlier. I really don't know. But my jaw drops more often than you can imagine.

Shortly after she turned three, Beth started attending the child alert program in Carmichaels. It was her first extensive foray on her own outside of the house. We would drive her down to the school and Dan Barger and Dolores Callahan would work with her, doing the fundamentals of speech therapy. It only lasted an hour or so and it was never easy. She was often tired or struggling health-wise and seemed to make little progress, but, looking back on that time, I think it was important in her developmental process. For the most part she liked it, which laid an important foundation for the years she would spend in school.

***

Beth also enjoyed playing with the chin-up bar that we put in one of our doorways. We used it to challenge the other girls to grow stronger. Carrie was the first of the three girls to win for herself a new Easter dress with her ability to do ten pull-ups. Only the ones where her arms were fully extended counted.

Beth, of course, couldn't even hold onto the bar, so weak were her hands, but she loved thinking that she could do what the others of us were doing. So I would hold her and do my best to get her hands to touch the bar at least and then lift her up and down. She seemed thrilled as if she were doing it all by herself.

To this day she gets vicarious excitement by watching TV shows that she cannot in any earthly way participate in. She loves to watch cooking shows on PBS: this from a girl who tastes almost nothing by mouth. And for some reason I can't get my head around completely, she will lie for hours with her iPad watching YouTube videos of folks doing various physical workouts. Again, this from a girl who can't sit unaided or stand unaided and has never taken a single step of any form. Yet there she lies watching the newest and best ways to get a flat stomach or to increase your aerobic strength. Sometimes she just flips from one to another. Ah, some of the distractions we find on the internet.

***

In November of 1989 we purchased our first mini-van, a white Chevy Astro. We had left Koinonia to begin our life in western Pennsylvania with two and a half kids (Merry was pregnant with Hannah) and a little Toyota Corolla. Four of us in that little car were just fine, five of us and we were feeling crowded. When Merry became pregnant with Beth, we knew we had to upgrade.

Living in the center of the coal and steel industries of this country, I was determined to buy an American car. So we bought a used Chrysler station wagon, one of the original K cars that saved Chrysler from bankruptcy. It was a great car, as had been the Toyota before it. But with Beth now having to be transported in her specially designed stroller, the station wagon was no longer adequate. We bought the Astro, removed the center seat and had some tie-downs installed to hold her in place.

That was the beginning of a succession of used vans specially equipped to meet Beth's needs. When a few years later she got her first power wheelchair, the Astro got replaced by a full size Ford F150 that had two beautiful captain's chairs in it when we purchased it. Unfortunately, none of us ever got to sit in them because we had to remove them so that we could install a handicapped lift to raise and lower her chair into the van.

That van gave way to another very similar in style. We drove both of them till they had about 175,000 miles on them. The last one got replaced soon after an accident in which only the hand of God kept us from serious injury. We were coming back from a week's vacation in Cape May, NJ, and were crossing the Walt Whitman Bridge coming back into Pennsylvania. We were in six lanes of traffic, three going each way, traveling about fifty-five miles an hour when the left front tie rod snapped.

I had never experienced anything like it. The car felt like it was a bucking bronco as the left wheel just flipped back and forth completely unattached to the steering mechanism. We were in the inside lane with two other family cars immediately behind us. Merry was changing Beth in the back, and she says that when she looked out the window all she saw was water, we were careening so violently. Miraculously, we were able to get the car stopped without hitting the bridge or being struck by another car. Within a couple of minutes three cop cars were attending to our situation. Within another five minutes a tow truck assigned full-time to the bridge was towing us off the bridge where another truck from AAA towed us to a local garage. The van up until that point had been totally reliable but, with that incident, I lost all confidence in it, and we were soon purchasing our first ever adapted minivan with lowered floor and fold out ramp, second hand, of course. Beth, who had always been behind us in the full-sized vans, now is able to drive her chair right up beside the driver, and we often travel hand in hand.

***

83

As I went out to sled ride with one of my granddaughters this afternoon, I was reminded of a note from Merry's journal about the first time (and one of the only times) we ever took Beth sled riding. As she has gotten older and bigger lugging her onto and off of a sled has become so much of an issue that we haven't done it in years. But when she was about three and a half, I took her down a fairly long hill with me.

I am not sure that, without knowing the intricacies of her physical condition, you can really get a grasp on what that meant for her, for me, for her family watching. There was a bit of terror in it for all of us, so many things that could go wrong, even on a simple sled ride. So we rehearsed it all, did our best to protect her from as many contingencies as we could imagine and finally took the plunge.

She absolutely loved it, laughed her sort of nervous laugh, where she is having a great time but more than a little scared, all the way down the hill.

That same spirit is evident in the whole family in a notation about Christmas of 1989 when Beth was about three and a half. My mom was beginning to show some serious effects from what we would discover about three months later was a brain tumor the size of an orange. That Christmas day lethargy was the most obvious issue. She did not wake up till after ten in the morning, while our four young ones waited patiently for grandma to rally so that they could open presents. While grandma stayed home, the rest of us took a walk around the parks in front of her home at 10:00 P.M. Taking an always fragile Beth on such a middle of the night escapade in winter was admittedly a bit of a stretch. But she loved it, seemed to pick up on the idea that this was something way out of the ordinary and that she was joining us on an adventure. Not much of an adventure by others' standards, but given her condition it was pretty wild by ours.

Two weeks later we celebrated the first anniversary of Beth's last visit to the hospital. Like the day she had been out of the hospital longer than she had been in it, this was a huge victory for our family. She had fought her way in that year through one cold after another, was most often very congested with mucous that she had difficulty clearing. But she hadn't been in the hospital, hadn't been away from the family and friends that meant so much to her and whose love was critical for her emotional as well as physical health.

But we were to go from that small miracle to the struggles of caring for my mom. Things were getting worse for her in a hurry and started becoming obvious to all. In one day, I received phone calls from three of Mom's closest friends telling me of weird things she was doing and saying. None of us had a clue what was going on and several trips to her doctors were only addressing the side issues like incontinence, instead of whatever was the root cause.

Mom's doctor assured us that it was just her old age, that his own mother was going through a very similar downward cycle. "I would only be wasting your money if we ran a bunch of tests," he assured me. After another round of calls from other friends, I called him up and said, "Waste my money." It would be a day or two before we got the results, but as I mentioned, it turned out to be a very large malignant brain tumor.

She did remarkably well through her surgery to remove it, developed something of a crush on the young doctor who performed the work and, after a serious setback from pulmonary embolisms that nearly killed her, came home to take up her normal routines for another ten years.

I mention all of that not to sidetrack us from Beth's story but to include this note. As she did with others who were hospitalized, Beth loved visiting her grandmother in the hospital. Perhaps it was because she had herself, at such a young age, discovered the joy of being visited. But this went well beyond anything she had known to date, because now she was allowed to sit up in bed beside grandma and help her open her get well cards. To this day, opening mail, none of which she can read or process in any significant way, except for a couple of magazines she receives monthly, is a huge deal for her.

***

At this stage of life with Beth, sleep was a huge issue. Merry notes in the journals that Tuesday, Thursday and Sunday were far and away the hardest days of the week for her to get through because they followed the nights on which she cared for Beth. We had brought her back upstairs into our bedroom with the hope that a more natural sleeping place would enable her to sleep better, and even more importantly, allow us to sleep together again for the first time in years. The experiment was not successful. Instead of one person ending up exhausted the next morning, we both were. Even as I type that sentence I am falling asleep at the keyboard, which I mention only to say that all these years later, not much has changed.

***

CHAPTER NINE

Swimming 1990 till Today

A T SOME POINT before she was four years old, we got comfortable enough with Beth's physical condition to try taking her swimming at the Waynesburg Central High School pool. This had for years been an activity that we had done as a family, often Dad and the girls going to give Mom a couple hours of peace. I would divide my time between the lap lane and the girls, who, before long, were joining me swimming laps.

Some likely would regard our taking Beth swimming as being irresponsible given her inabilities to protect her air passage and her general floppiness in the pool. Merry was not quite of that opinion, but she simply could not be around Beth in the water. Every time Beth took in some water, which was not infrequently, Merry was sure that would be the onset of pneumonia, if not immediate drowning.

We tried all kinds of expensive devices to help her keep her head out of the water, but the only one she has ever been comfortable with were a regular pair of kids' "floaties" that we would blow up and put on her arms. She was really quite adept at keeping her head above water with them.

While she preferred being in an upright position as if she were treading water, I was quite insistent that like the rest of us she needed to get some exercise and would make her get on her back and sweep her arms to propel herself the length of the pool. I would swim in front of her, occasionally lifting her head if it looked like she was going to put it under water or steering her if one arm was pulling her to the side instead of straight ahead. She got fairly proficient at swimming a full lap, one length of the pool up and back. A later journal note describes the first time she went "under" intentionally. I think she had seen her sisters and me swimming underwater and wanted to try it out. She would put her head in the water and pull it back but wanted more than that. With her floaties (and sometimes other flotation devices on) she actually could not get herself under, so I started practicing with her. I would grab her and say "ready" and then quickly pull her under and back up again. She loved it, thought she was hot stuff.

I mention this because it reminds me how over the years Merry and I have had some things that each of us could handle better than the other. I could handle the swimming and have always been more comfortable than Merry just letting Beth drive off in her chair, really most anywhere she wants to go. She usually doesn't go far even to this day, but Merry is much more comfortable when she is in her line of sight. Other things Merry is much more relaxed about than I am. For both of us finding that fine line between being overly protective and allowing her freedom to explore the world for herself is an ongoing struggle.

Both of us over the years have become really quite comfortable letting her go completely on her own in big stores like Target, her favorite because of its wide aisles, or Walmart, a close second. When we make our annual pilgrimage to Oklahoma to visit our eldest daughter, Emily, and her family who settled there more than twelve years ago now, it is something of a ritual that Beth and I go to Super Target with Em's husband Matt. Matt and I most often have a list of shopping to do and sometimes Beth will stay with us for part of that time, but more often than not she is off zooming up and down the aisles checking out her favorite items (notebooks, usually small colorful ones, are her favorite.)

When we go to the beach most every summer together, Matt will often take Beth for a morning to Walmart or Target just to hang out with her. Beth loves being with her family at the beach, but, like her dad, she does not like sitting in the sand hanging out. So we are often found walking up and down the boardwalk. Or someone, like Matt, will take her somewhere to entertain her, while the rest of the clan is in the water or hanging out. For the curious, we have seldom tried ocean swimming for Beth which definitely feels like it would be over the top risky.

***

The writing of this book has been erratic. It requires time to read the old journals and then to write. And emotional energy to process a lot of this stuff that we have not dredged up for years. I guess we have left it in the past not wanting to recall a lot of it. So I go months in between writing sections and as I take this up again after a spring and summer relapse I realize the whole swimming issue has been at the center of this year's summer as well.

In July of 2015, while I was off with some folks from the church on a missions trip to Kentucky building accessible ramps for folks in need, Beth and her aide went swimming in the Waynesburg public pool. At one point her aide pulled her under a rope to go from one section to another, a routine we have certainly done plenty of times before. All we can figure is that Beth breathed in when she should have breathed out. We will likely never know, shy of heaven, exactly what happened. But she turned blue almost immediately and was carried by the director of Parks and Recreation, Jake Blaker, into a room where lifeguards and other personnel administered CPR while an ambulance was called.

Incredibly, present at the pool that day with her kids was a cardiac/pulmonary nurse from Ruby Memorial Hospital in Morgantown who quickly joined in the efforts to revive her and the local paramedics responded with lightning speed. They could not get a pulse, though Beth never has a strong pulse and her heart is actually around on the side of her body, not near the center of the chest cavity because of her scoliosis. Did her heart stop? We'll never know, but at the least the medical experts at the scene felt it had. Beth revived quickly and was transported to the Greene County Airport where she was life-flighted to UPMC Presbyterian.

In Kentucky, I got this frantic call from my wife, "Something happened to Beth at the pool. They are life-flighting her. I'll call when I know more." I called a good friend, Charlie Anderson, and asked him to get to the airport and see if there was any way he could help, which he graciously agreed to do. Then sitting on the tailgate of a truck, I let go and cried. The whole team gathered and prayed and we decided to leave Kentucky for home that evening after work instead of waiting as planned to go the next morning.

Sometime in the midst of a flurry of calls that then went on the rest of that day, I thought to call another good friend, Tom Ribar, formerly the chaplain of Waynesburg University, who is now living in Pittsburgh. (Tom and his wife Tami have been good friends for years and she was one of Beth's occupational therapists when she was much younger.) I asked him to go to Presby to see if he could add any emotional and spiritual support to Merry. Hannah and her eleven month old daughter, Clara, were visiting so they drove up to the hospital.

Hannah tells a great story of arriving at about the same time as Tom. Merry and Beth were back in the ER surrounded by a team of doctors trying to figure out if she needed any help. Hannah and Tom went to the desk to ask if they could go back to see Beth. They got directed to a social worker. Very professionally, this caring lady explained that in moments of trauma like this, people often don't want to see visitors, so that they should be very reserved and kind of feel Beth out as to how she was feeling. She agreed to let Hannah and Clara go in, but told Tom that she would play it by ear, and if Beth showed any hesitation about Tom's presence she would have to ask him to leave.

What the dear lady failed to have any kind of grasp of was Beth's love of attention directed her way, especially by good-looking men. So as they were walking back towards the room, the social worker, Hannah and Clara and Tom, Beth caught sight of them and yelled out this loud, enthusiastic greeting, "Tom Ribar!" Needless to say, he was not asked to leave.

By the time I arrived the next morning to take them home, Beth was asking if she could stay. The constant attention from nurses and young doctors was something very special and she had already charmed the pants off most of them. Several actually broke away from their rounds briefly to come and say goodbye to her when we were leaving.

***

Another "big" event of this summer of 2015 coincides with a note from Merry's journal of May 1990. There twenty-six years ago, at the age of four, Beth began to serve as a greeter at our Sunday morning worship services, a job she has performed faithfully just about every Sunday since then. She sits just inside the door in her power chair, eagerly waiting to hand out a bulletin to, and hoping for hugs from, anyone who enters the door. We, of course, also assign some other adults to do the same job and greet folks as they enter the sanctuary. Often times, if those folks are doing their job well, their friendly greetings capture the attention of worshippers before they see Beth tucked away in the corner and they go right on by her. It doesn't seem to faze her, though she gets a special thrill when folks will take a bulletin from her. When we, three or four times a year, visit other churches as a part of our Ministerium's special services, she always asks me, "Dad, who is doing the greeting?" hoping

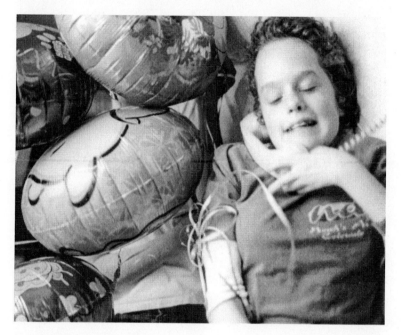

that she can worm her way into the job. And more times than not, my fellow pastors are more than glad for her to be a part of the greeting team.

This summer our church finally recognized another weekly service that Beth has performed for years. When the ushers finish collecting the offering each week, they pile the plates on Beth's lap and she drives the offering to the front of the church and hands it off to whoever is there receiving it. She then backs up the aisle its entire length without ever looking back to see where she is going. If that does not impress you, just try it sometime you are around a power wheelchair that is sitting empty. She is a wizard with that chair.

Anyway, this summer the church nominating committee nominated Beth to serve as an official usher. She doesn't officially take office until January and it will mean nothing more than what she had been doing for a decade or more but she was totally thrilled to be asked. She had to call her sisters immediately to tell them and went around telling everyone for at least two weeks that she was going to be an usher.

***

Back in the summer of 1990, while Beth was first polishing her swimming and taking up new roles of service in the church, Emily and Carrie, along with nine others from our church family, made a trip to Tijuana, Mexico to be a part of Habitat for Humanity's Jimmy Carter Work Project there, building one hundred homes in a week. Though I think the week was really formative for my two girls, it gets mentioned here because in our first hours at the site, I stepped on a piece of reinforcing wire that penetrated my foot. Despite treating the wound immediately and taking the strongest oral antibiotics available, I ended up having surgery on it when I got home and spending several days in the hospital. Then I was on IV antibiotics at home for two weeks when I got out. None of that was much of a big deal, except that it meant I nearly missed Beth's fourth birthday party, and birthday parties and Beth are a big deal. I guess it is another case of her being the center of everyone's attention, more so than most any other time. She loves them.

***

That thought evokes another, a sense of guilt that I know plagues both Merry and me even to this day. Our lives are very busy. Years ago it was work and homeschooling and

getting the girls where they needed to be with all the things they were doing. Today it is still work and now Merry is a tax collector for our borough and a late blooming artist as well as gardener for the entire church grounds. As much as possible, we keep Beth busy and by our side.

I will take her visiting shut-ins with me or down to the trail to run or walk beside me. And Merry has her out in the garden or walking with her to the Post Office or folding washcloths (she's a pro at that.)

But a lot of the time, there are things that we need to do or want to do and Beth can't or simply does not want to do with us, and she gets left lying on her gurney watching TV or watching something on her iPad. Even when we do have time to spend with her, it is often difficult to figure out what we should do. We try puzzles which sometimes she really enjoys, and games, again sometimes she really likes them, and reading (that works well at night or at nap time but almost never just in the middle of the day.) Anyway, a lot of the time she lies there watching something and Merry and I feel guilty but don't know how to break that cycle.

***

CHAPTER TEN

New Tools of Accessibility 1990

IN AUGUST OF 1990, we took Bethany to Children's Hospital yet again, this time for a barium swallow test. Since birth she had been tube fed, but as she got older and some muscles seemed to develop a bit, we held out hope that her swallowing mechanisms might yet improve to the point that she could eat by mouth. Face it, eating is such a huge part of all of our lives that it was hard to give up hope that our fourth daughter would be allowed such a fundamental joy of life.

The test involved having her attempt to swallow this radioactive glob that looked a bit like yogurt. Then the dye gets traced by x-rays that help us see exactly where the food is going. Beth ended up being unable to breathe, turning blue and gagging all of the barium up. The folks doing the test had to call for an emergency response team to help clear her. So the test was a bust, except that Dr. Zitelli witnessed it and concluded that it was a muscle spasm that would not let anything go down. Because that was not a voluntary muscle, it was not possible to aid its development. He concluded that there was no hope of her learning to eat. Clearly we were disappointed, though also grateful that at least she did not get any of the stuff in her lungs, which had been a major concern

in doing the test, and did not develop pneumonia.

Four days after that test, obviously not giving up on the idea entirely, Merry notes that we tried giving Beth a bottle to drink but that she was not interested. Over the years she has moments when she has tried to sip some water reasonably successfully. She will often ask for water saying, "Man, I'm thirsty," wanting more than anything to be like everyone else. But she rarely drinks it.

***

A note from August of that year reminds me of two foundational principles that have been a part of Beth's life from the get go and remain so even today. First, as a family, we have made every effort to include her in as much of our life as humanly possible. Secondly, God gave her a mom who is one heck of a woman.

We had at some point bought an oversized backpack designed to carry a large child. Merry and I had transported all of our kids in their early months in front packs and back packs, and we reasoned Beth was small enough that even at four years we might be able to take her hiking with us. One summer day we went for a family hike near Coopers Rock in West Virginia. Beth's lack of muscle strength meant that she was always sliding down in the back pack so we would position her with pillows or extra jackets or whatever to keep her reasonably straight, but she was always uncomfortable. Because she could not support herself well and was slipping around on my back, her weight was an awkward carry and my back got sore more quickly than it might otherwise. And, as you likely have guessed, we got lost, so were several hours hiking up and down the hills and valleys of the state park. Ouch! Beth and I were both about toast when we finally made it to the car and I am not sure we ever used that expensive back pack again.

But never one to say die, on another trip, this one to Ohio Pyle, Merry strapped her on her front and carried her first down to the river's edge and then to Cucumber Falls. What a woman!

***

Up until this time Beth had been pushed around in a specially designed stroller. We would lift her in and out of the stroller to put her in our minivan when we traveled, folding the stroller up and putting it in the back. On August 16, we went to New Kensington where she was fitted for the first time for a manual wheelchair which she herself could push around. Looking back on it from the distance of a quarter century, it seems like an impossible dream. But we have never been sure what her physical and mental capabilities are. Certainly at the time we had visions of her having a relatively independent life pushing herself around in her chair like some of these remarkably fit paraplegics. It was not to be, of course, but how could we know that at the time? Doctors had always said to us that, though we do not add muscle tissue as we mature, what muscles we have can grow stronger with exercise. That was our hope for Beth. This chair also had the first of several contour seats designed specifically to fit the curvature of her spine. She was fitted for that seating at the Children's Rehab Institute, a place we would come to love for its incredibly caring and gracious staff. Our daughter Hannah would work there when her husband was doing his residency in family medicine at UPMC while they were awaiting the birth of their first child.

The manual chair was not a total bust. It reclined, which was very helpful because Beth was often chokey, and reclining her saved the time and work of lifting her out of the chair to lie her down. And the truth is that she could push herself around somewhat. Her getting this chair became an impetus to have the carpets in the church parsonage, which Merry never liked, but which had been installed just before we moved in, taken up and the hardwood floors resurfaced. In those early days, because of the carpet at the house, we would take Beth over to the big open tiled floor of the church educational building so she could push herself around. Of course, any incline, up or down was trouble.

That chair was also the beginning of several major changes in our life and the life of our church family. Seeing her in that chair made it finally sink in for all of us that her condition was not something that was going to get better, but was something we could make more comfortable for all of us. So for instance, we got ramps to push her into and out of the van, without lifting her out of her chair into another seat, and tie downs to secure the chair once it was in the van.

And the church began work on a ramp at the front of the church for her to be able to worship without a couple of people having to lift the chair up the steps. A ramp fund had actually been started years before with a donation from an elderly lady in the congregation, Lottie Ankrom, but hadn't gone anywhere. But with Beth in a chair, there became a very clear sense that this was something that needed to happen. So the work began.

It would not be long before there was a ramp installed into the back of the building as well and years later a handicap-accessible push-pad so that Beth and others could get in and out of a rather heavy steel door. What an incredible blessing both of those projects have been for many in our church. By the time the front ramp was completed, another young boy in a wheelchair was regularly attending worship and participated with Beth and Lottie in cutting the ribbon when we had a dedication service for the ramp.

***

Incredibly three weeks after the church dedicated the ramp for the front of the church, trustees and other volunteers set to work on a wooden ramp (that has since been replaced by a permanent cement ramp) to make it possible for us to wheel Beth in and out of the parsonage. Until then we had pulled her backwards up the six or seven steps to the back door.

That was the first of many projects the church family undertook to make life in our home more accessible for Beth and easier for the rest of us. It would be another ten years or more, but eventually an addition to the parsonage would be built that would make possible a bedroom on the first floor for Beth.

As part of that addition, a room in the house that had been a study when we first moved in, and that had served as a homeschool classroom for most of our years, was converted into an accessible bathroom. It is impossible to overestimate how the roll-in shower that was a part of that conversion has eased our life. When we go on vacation or travel anywhere else, we end up putting off giving her a real shower till we get home. A good friend, George Kelley, who had cared for our cars with incredible and generous abilities, took an old bath chair that we had purchased years before to place in a bath tub and built a roll-in component to it that we have used for more than almost twenty years now. What a blessing!

The roll-in shower and bath chair remind me of a recent happening that might give you a glimpse into life with Beth and the joy that it can give. The shower head that was first installed in that new shower recently got clogged from sediment to the point that it was emitting a very small amount of water, not enough to get much beyond Beth's face as she sat in the bath chair. It was totally unsatisfactory, but in the busyness of life, I just kept putting off getting it fixed. Beth, who totally loves the PBS show "This Old House," started saying every morning as we took our shower, "We need to call Kevin O'Connor (the host of the show) and get 'This Old House' down here to fix that." Morning after morning for months on end, I would hear that same refrain and even started saying it myself. Finally disgusted with the situation, I walked across the street and asked my good friends Bill Watson and Chuck Coles from Watson and Son Plumbing (whose office and warehouse is right across the street from our home) what I could do about it. They said simply, "We'll take care of it," and the next day they came over and did a complete overhaul of the shower head and the detachable shower hose that went with it. (They never sent us a bill for labor or materials.) The water flowed with strength and volume once again and we loved it. Beginning that morning and continuing for months afterwards, Beth began to say, "We don't need Kevin O'Connor. We have the Watson boys."

***

Bethany continued her regular trips going to "school" at the Child Alert program in Carmichaels, about seven miles away. Merry had been, initially, understandably nervous about letting her go into the care of van drivers and teachers who did not know anything about her condition and how to care for her if something went wrong. So she set out to write a multi-page letter detailing everything that could go wrong and what to do for her if it did. It was really a very helpful aid but you can perhaps imagine the panic it set off in the hearts and minds of drivers and teachers who had no training or experience in dealing with life threatening issues like Beth's. I think they all freaked out, at least until we met with them and explained that, while these things could happen, they almost never did and that for the most part she was relatively stable. Meanwhile, Beth was busy charming them all and many became and remain to this day close friends of the family.

***

In September of that year, I took Beth and Hannah and Carrie and her friend Melissa Thorne to the Arboretum in Pittsburgh. I mention this only because, unimaginable by anyone at that time, Melissa would die of cancer shortly after graduating from high school. While we lived with the possibility of Beth dying any day, the truth is that that same thing is true for everyone. Death is an ever constant threat to all life. We just usually don't give it much thought. I think that our years with Beth gave us a special sensitivity to Melissa's suffering and that of her family. But it was also certainly the case that anytime a young person would get ill or go to the hospital, we would be somewhat dismissive, figuring that Beth's sufferings were greater and that she would certainly die first. I would like to think that Beth has been used by God to care for a host of families in our community in ways that we likely would have missed had it not been for our time with her.

***

On November 6 of 1990, for the first time in our married life, we had an old TV brought into the house and hooked it up to an old antenna that had been on the roof when we moved in. Until then our TV watching had been limited to times when we visited my mom in Waynesburg or when we would go next door to the church to watch a VCR tape. The TV's entrance into our lives was one of our concessions to life with a physically challenged child who could not entertain herself by running and playing as easily as our three older daughters. Emily, Carrie and Hannah were fifteen, twelve and eight when we got that first TV and I don't think that they regret at all those years of not having one.

Fifteen years later we would make a further concession. We paid a very good friend and incredibly talented electronics guy, Allen Fox, to install a new antenna which has provided a number of channels and much more reliable signal than the previous one. But PBS and particularly Mr. Roger's Neighborhood and Sesame Street were for years the staples of our TV viewing. They made it seem like it was always "a beautiful day in this neighborhood."

***

CHAPTER ELEVEN

New Possibilities 1991

IN JANUARY OF 1991 we had one of our very rare negative encounters with a doctor at Children's Hospital. Our friend and trusted advisor, Dr. Tim Ward, who saw Beth for all things orthopedic, which primarily concerned her spine, must have been having a bad day. Hey, we all have them, but we somehow expect that doctors should not. He was cold and somewhat disrespectful in a manner that was not like him at all. We were to see Dr. Zitelli after our visit with him and took the occasion to vent a little about our negative encounter. To this day, I don't know if Basil spoke to Ward about our complaints or not, but that evening Dr. Ward called us at our home and apologized for having been so unpleasant, a move that forever sealed our respect for the man.

***

I have mentioned previously how much Beth loves babies and that her absolute favorite hospital visit with me is to go see a newborn. I have no idea how many babies and their families we have visited, but she has held every one, had her picture taken with most and wanted to stay far longer than was appropriate with each one.

It is always a time of reflection for me knowing that in a few years time each child will surpass Beth in mental and physical functions. It is most notable, of course, with our own grandchildren whom she is so nurturing towards and who, within such a short period of time, are relating to her as if they are the grown-up. The first baby we have a record of her visiting was Louie Pellegrini whom we visited on January 12, 1991. Louie is now a physical therapist and is incredibly gracious to Beth when we see him, which happens most Wednesdays when Beth goes to swim at the Wellness Center where he is working.

***

Merry notes on January 18 of that year, "Beth needs more discipline." Say it ain't so...Wow! That is to this day probably the most difficult thing about parenting her. The sleepless nights, the lack of time together as a couple, the years of giving up our own agendas to care for her: none of that compares in difficulty or stress with the issues related to discipline.

Fortunately, most folks don't see a lot of her nastiness. And I suppose we should be grateful that with all of her physical restrictions and the near constant pain that she lives in, she is not a whole lot worse. But this sweet angelic little handicapped young woman can spout a really horrific, "I hate you, Dad." And like most youngsters, she knows when to try to get away with it: when we are already late getting out the door or when visitors are about to walk in the door. I am not sure she has the mental clarity to actually think it through, but it seems like her tantrums are often at the most inconvenient times. Likely they are the result of stress that one or the other or both of us are experiencing . So her lack of control is probably symptomatic of our own lack of peace.

I also get glimpses every now and then about how I am more than a little responsible. We can have spent a great three or four hours together on a hospital visit or some such outing. We get home and I am ready to move on to something else. Merry will not be taking over Beth's care as fast as I would like, and I will say or do something with Beth that indicates my impatience. And she, right now, is angry and spouting venom. There is absolutely no reasoning with her. Sometimes time-out works to give her a few minutes to clear her head and refocus. But just as often it doesn't work. I will probably get arrested for admitting it, but we have slapped her arm or leg. It never succeeded in doing anything other than making her more volatile. We pray about it and long for some sign of progress. But that journal entry could have been written today just as easily as twenty-five years ago.

***

That summer a friend, Jerry Bailey, who operated heavy equipment, graciously bulldozed a level spot on the piece of property up the hill where we went sled riding in the winter. We loved going up there for cook outs or to play games, but the entire piece of ground was fairly steep. Beth couldn't be put down anywhere or left unattended in her chair. Refusing to take any money for his work, Jerry changed that completely. Another good friend, Rick Bartoletti, (a multi-talented man who has become my most consistent kayaking partner) shortly thereafter spent the better part of a day on his front end loader carving a pathway that weaved across the property so that Beth could drive up and down the hillside. We should have paved it because it was never smooth enough for her to drive comfortably, but it functioned as a way she could hang out with all of us when we were up there.

***

In March of 1992, Merry had a dream about Bethany being with Jesus. The dream was filled with happiness and light and love and Mer woke up sobbing with joy. The reality of heaven has burned ever so much brighter for all of us because of our years with Beth, knowing as we do what a total blessing it will be for her.

***

That same month Beth began to use a scooter board. It consisted of a board about two feet long, somewhat padded with four wheels under it. She would lie on it on her stomach and use her arms to push herself around the house. One of those many babies that we had visited came for a visit to our house one day when she had just begun to crawl. Beth was so fascinated by her crawling that she asked to get on her scooter and proceeded to push herself around for almost an hour, a Herculean accomplishment for one so very weak.

In the summer of 1992 we made what became our almost annual pilgrimage to the shore at Cape May, N.J. I had gone there with my parents and siblings a number of times growing up, had worked there two summers of my college years and have now taken kids and grandkids there on and off for more than two decades.

Our great discovery of that year was the surf chairs that the community provided for kids like Beth. They were essentially her bath chair on huge balloon tires. We loved them because it made it possible for Beth to join the family at the water's edge instead of remaining hundreds of feet away on the boardwalk. (Wheelchairs, powered or manual, merely sink in the sand.)

My favorite thing to do at the beach has always been to walk or run right along the surf and suddenly I could include Beth in that activity. We would take long walks, often gaining special dispensation from the generous lifeguards in whose care the chairs rested, so that we were able to keep the chair long after the guards left the beach for the day.

As the years went by and Beth's scoliosis got worse, the chairs worked less well. If she went in them without her brace, the back pain soon became excruciating. If we left the brace on, she soon became uncomfortably hot. But for a time those chairs were a huge blessing.

It was on one of those early trips to Cape May when Beth was still in her manual chair that we experienced a powerful work of God's grace to us. Beth was on the porch, six or seven steps up, of the house we were staying in, saying goodbye to some friends who had been visiting. Somehow the brakes on her chair came loose and she rolled off the

porch. I was standing on the sidewalk immediately in front of the chair and must have caught a glimpse of it out of the corner of my eye. My instinct was to duck and so Beth rolled over my back, still in her chair, banged her head off the steps and somehow was OK, with some bumps and bruises, but no serious injuries.

***

On August 31, 1992, Beth became a part of the Jefferson-Morgan school system for the first time as she ventured into a special ed classroom in the elementary school. Nancy McClaren was her first teacher there and remained so for a number of years. Beth loved those days. We still have an old VHS tape that they made where kids all brought in different objects that began with a certain letter of the alphabet (totally boring to you and me), but totally engrossing to Beth still today. In fact, in the days we were proofing this text, out of the blue, she spotted it on the shelf and asked to watch it.

***

In the winter of 1993, our sanctuary was being replastered and repainted, so for a number of weeks we gathered in a large circle in our educational building. It was actually an interesting time because the smaller, more confined space was much more intimate than the larger sanctuary and seemed to amplify congregational singing. We managed to attract several folks to worship who likely would never have come to a service in the more formal setting of the sanctuary, including Jefferson's only homeless man, Jim Miller. Jim is one of the hardest working people you will ever meet, but his situation does not lend itself to everyday cleanliness. The truth is he often looked and acted a bit wild. It mattered not to Beth when he came through the door. She zoomed over in her chair and immediately took his hand and led him into the worship circle. He didn't stay with us long, but I could only wonder, if more of us had greeted him with Beth's enthusiasm would it have made a difference?

***

Everyone in our family loves to read, though no one more than my wife. It has been a point of tension in our marriage at times, because she reads so much faster than I do and so reads ten times as many books in a year as I do. And in case I haven't mentioned this yet, I am highly competitive about all such things.

Beth, of course, has never read well, much to all of our disappointment. We think how richer and fuller her life might be if she could at least entertain herself with reading. She never got beyond the most elementary "Dick and Jane" series and now doesn't even do those. Stories don't interest her anything like people do. A book on tape is soon boring for her, but a YouTube video of a baby laughing can entertain her for hours.

BUT one thing she got at a very early age was the ability to identify store signs. She can pick out a Target or Walmart store before anyone in the car. Twenty-three years ago she was saying "cookie" when she would see an Eat'n Park sign and would sing the jingle for us.

***

Beth has also always known exactly what she wanted, though she often will sucker the rest of us as we wait to find out just what that is. One night she was calling out from her room as we were watching TV in the living room. It is a nightly affair (no matter what we are doing, watching, reading, eating.) Every so often she will call out for someone to roll her over. On this occasion, she was calling out, "Someone, hey, someone!" When Merry got up and went in saying, "Yes?" Beth responded, "Not you, Mom, I mean Dad!"

***

CHAPTER TWELVE

Establishing Traditions 1994-1996

O N JUNE 17, 1994 it was time for us to apply for a new handicapped placard for parking. One of the greatest frustrations of transporting Beth in the van is finding a spot to park when we arrive at our destination. Most places have way too few spots designated for handicapped parking; that's a part of the problem. But the thing that drives me crazy is the places at stores like Walmart that set aside these huge areas for van parking that are really sweet if you ever get one, because you can unload Beth in her chair without fear that the ramp is going to bang another car or that she won't have room to turn once she gets off the ramp. They are awesome, but it seems like nine out of ten times that I pull up to one there is this tiny little car, that has no need whatsoever for such a spot, parked in it.

Folks in charge of such designations need to reserve, in my humble opinion, spots that are designed for van access to van access. I don't begrudge a spot near the door for those who have difficulty walking, but please don't park in the only spots where I can get my kid in and out without difficulties.

***

That summer also began a tradition that has continued almost every year since then of taking Beth for a day, or at least a few hours, to Kennywood. She tires quickly, so we cram in as much as we can as fast as we can and get out before she crashes completely. Praise God for the help places like Kennywood give to those with disabilities in letting us go to

the front of the line and stay on the ride twice without getting off. It is a tremendous blessing.

Beth, for all of her physical frailty, has something of an indomitable spirit. So on her first trip to Kennywood, she rode the Log Jammer (which has certainly become her favorite ride over the years) four times, Raging Rapids twice, the Bumper cars four times. Since then she has added the Racer, the Pittsburgh Plunge, the Jack Rabbit and a few

115

others. We all vie for the spots next to her on the ride, because it is just such a total delight to watch her joy in sharing in the family fun. Well, we all vie for those spots except those of us not as brave as Beth.

On that first trip, after overcoming some understandable jitters, she took that initial trip on the Log Jammer. She acted terrified through the whole first trip and then begged to do it

again, and again, and with each time the ride was repeated, she gained confidence and enjoyed it all the more.

Her love for the Log Jammer is now rivaled by a couple of roller coaster rides and what is perhaps the family favorite, the Raging Rapids. For those familiar with the ride, there is a point where the boat you are in spins out of control and one portion plunges directly beneath a deluge of a waterfall. Beth loves being the one who gets totally soaked, and even enjoys getting nailed a second time in a row. In the minutes after the ride, we all begin to pay the price, however. By then she is sitting in sopping wet clothes, cold and miserable, until we take her somewhere and get her changed. But the misery of the after-ride is quickly forgotten and, by the time the next year's trip rolls around, she is ever so eager to do it again. Her zeal for such excitement in the face of all it means for her in terms of discomfort and pain is nothing short of inspiring.

Inspired by our success with Beth on the Raging Rapids, and with a desire to visit eldest daughter Emily who was that summer working at Noah's Ark, a Christian white water rafting company in Buena Vista, CO, we traveled west. Emily insisted that we all go down the river with her as our guide. I balked. Merry was much more ready to give it a whirl. I explained to Emily, and other members of the staff that she brought in to convince me, that if Beth were to go in the white water, no matter how well we had her secured in a life jacket, it would mean certain death. The staff were convinced that they could keep her safe and, when I finally relented, put our boat in a pod with other boats directed by their very best guides. We all survived and by now you can guess who had the best time. Anytime Beth got the least bit nervous, we would just shriek, "It's the Logjammer," and she would be fine. I was terrified the whole time. She loved it.

***

While I was reading through the journal for 1994, Jennifer Zeo, a family friend and for a time one of Beth's aides, came to the house to say goodbye. We hadn't been in touch for a while and were surprised to learn that she and her family were moving back to Florida where they had lived before moving into the Jefferson area probably ten years ago. I mention this only because, though we had been friends, I am quite certain she would not have come by to say goodbye to Merry and me. In fact, she said as she came in the door, "I had to come to say goodbye to Beth." Merry and I just smiled at each other as the two visited together for maybe half an hour.

We both remembered thinking twenty years prior, "What will folks remember most when we are gone about our years of ministry in Jefferson? We both concluded then, and Jennifer's visit seemed to confirm it to us both, that they will most remember Beth.

***

On October 17, we again visited Dr. Ward who measured her lower curve at 109 degrees and her upper one at 64 degrees. He marveled, as we do, that she can sit at all and that she is not in excruciating pain. In typical Beth style, she insisted on giving Dr. Ward and his assistant a hug before we left.

***

On Halloween that year Merry took Beth to Mary Bargerstock's house and brought along candy for the two of them to hand out together. Mary was something of a social outcast whom kids and adults alike treated with disrespect. Her husband had been unbalanced mentally towards the end of his life, writing "Property of U.S. government" in red spray paint across the front of his house.

The house itself was dilapidated beyond any possible restoration. I organized the churches in our community to raise money for materials to build a new home for her and then put together the crew to do the actual work of construction. Mary took great pride in her new home and really put her life in order, becoming a regular member of our local Nazarene church. She was totally thrilled to have someone take the interest in her to come and share the fun of handing out candy to trick-or treaters. She and Beth together on the front porch were a big hit with the community. They laughed together a lot that evening.

***

On November 8th we began another round of the antibiotic Augmentin for the third time in two months. That was fairly typical, even when Beth was reasonably healthy. That left lung was just forever becoming infected as it was not properly inflating, all due to the muscle weakness with which she was born and the increasing scoliosis.

***

In January of 1995, it was my turn to do the rounds of teachers at the school to get a progress report on Beth's work. Three different teachers, her regular special ed teacher, a speech teacher and the assistant principal all regaled me with stories, most of which focused on how Beth did everything in her power to avoid doing school work. Her two most common techniques were faking sickness, (she was sick so often you sort of had to buy into it, at least initially), and simply driving away when you were giving her instructions. That can be kind of cute if you are watching it happen to another adult, but downright frustrating if you are the one trying to command her attention.

She did it to me just the other day when I was coming up out of my office in the church basement and she, who had been waiting for me to come for several minutes, drove off around the garage. I just let her go after trying to get her to come talk to me. I stopped to talk with Merry who was sitting under her rose trellis. Several minutes went by and we both realized we hadn't seen Beth in a while. We started calling, looked around the garage, inside the church, talked to our neighbor, George Shipley, with whom she regularly visits. I finally hopped on my bike and was sailing down the alley when I looked over and out of the corner of my eye caught sight of her. She was pulled into another neighbor's garage and was entertaining him with our plans for the next several days. She had assured him that I was coming to pick her up to take her visiting with me. We were going visiting, but we had certainly not made any such arrangement.

***

A special shout-out goes to the aforementioned George Shipley. George and his wife, Darlene, are our nearest neighbors and just about every day, often times more than once, when the weather is nice, Beth will be out looking for George. Most often washing one of his vehicles or pulling weeds from his gravel driveway, George will dutifully stop what he is doing when he sees her, come over and give her the mandatory hug and the two will talk about the weather or something equally mundane. "It's a hot one today, George," is a line that Beth repeats multiple times a day, even when just calling across the yard to him. But he has been one of her most loyal and consistent friends.

***

That winter, as most, we made it to as many boys' and girls' basketball games as we could. They are great times to encourage kids playing and to visit with their parents. Beth spends most of the time these days driving around in the lobby, but when her sisters were playing ball, and all three of them did, she was right there in the front row.

She often asked if she could hand the ball to the ref so that he could hand the ball to the team with the first possession. After doing that a number of times with one referee, he came one night with a small basketball for her to keep. Guess who was excited about that.

On April 8 of that year, Merry's journal notes that she found Carrie crying because she wasn't spending enough time with Beth. We all felt that way then and still today. We live such crazy busy lives.

That's part of it. The other part is that she is not easy to spend time with. Occasionally we can get her to play a game with us if we are really insistent about it. Sometimes she will do a puzzle with us.

At bedtime or nap time we can read to her as she is falling asleep, but no other time. She will watch TV gladly, but that is such an impersonal connection, and there is very little that she wants to watch that any of the rest of us wants to watch. I often make her go on a walk with me; but just hanging out talking with her, like you would with any other thirty year old, that just doesn't happen much. It is another reason I take her to do hospital visits with me. It gives Merry a break from the pressure of "What am I going to do with Beth next," and compels me to spend some time talking with her, which usually means answering a string of questions from her.

***

Beth has always had an affinity for others who have their own special needs. Our local Greene County Habitat for Humanity built an accessible house up the street from us that Glenn and Dorothy Snyder moved into. Glenn had been in a wheelchair for years after a bad car wreck. The Snyders had a big caring family, but for several reasons, most notably Glenn's inability to get around much, they didn't have a lot of friends in the local community. Enter Beth. She loved visiting them, calling them on the phone, just loving on them.

I think she saw their need in a way that I never did and served to bring our family closer with them in a way that would never have happened without her.

***

We still had a church choir back in those days. Beth loves music and enjoys singing, but her favorite part of choir practice each week was being allowed to hand out and gather up the music. She has such a helpful spirit. It gives her such joy to be able to help out. Sometimes at choir she would be rather withdrawn: maybe it was fatigue, maybe she was disgruntled about something, and maybe she just felt the inward need for some space, like all of us do at times. But just as often, she would be so animated and ready to chatter away with anyone and everyone that she would be totally disruptive of practice and you would love to have had a switch to shut off the motor mouth.

***

Every six weeks or so, I will roast some raw almonds in the oven and then get Beth to put them away in a gallon jar. She often does it one nut at a time, but loves doing it, does not find it boring, is just so grateful for a job where she can help out. "Are you proud of me, Daddy?" she will ask. (Aw, there is another occasion when she calls me Daddy.)

For years, once a week, Andi Kush, a therapist from the Pittsburgh area, would come down and work with Beth, stretching her and trying to increase, or at least hold steady whatever mobility she had. Andi became a part of the family, and, though we haven't seen her now for well more than two decades, we still get cards from her and other reminders that she is still thinking of her time with Beth and all the rest of us.

***

On March 13, 1996 a young man, Kurt Leighty, who had grown up in our church and had been classmates with our eldest daughter, Emily, died in a car crash. I took the early morning phone call and was asked to go give the news to his

grandmother, who also was active in the church and lived just a couple of blocks away. Merry and I both got so involved in caring for the Leighty family that morning that we both spaced out that it was the day we routinely had Beth dropped off from school at the Senior Citizen Center where I wash dishes. It is a time for me to catch up with some folks I don't see at any other time and Beth always loves zooming around talking to folks. For years I did it every week, but presently have gotten tied up with other commitments that limit my time to once or twice a month. So that day someone from the center had to walk her home or they loaded her back on the bus or somehow she got home, without any input from us.

Kurt's death affected us profoundly not only because we felt the pain of his parents, but because it caused us to reflect once again on the fleeting nature of life. We had spent much of the last ten years, now thirty years, preparing for our child's death and then in an instant, out of the blue, with no warning, no preparation, another life is taken. The secret things belong to the Lord our God.

***

The spring of 1996 was a time of life getting easier for Bethany, in large part due to the wonderful care of our church family at Jefferson Baptist. They first organized for us a van fund that allowed us, in March, to purchase our first full-sized van with a lift installed in it so that we could more easily transport her. Many generous donations came in, and we tried as best we could to get a picture of Beth getting into the van to everyone who contributed.

Just a few weeks later at the spring church business meeting the church voted to make one of the bathrooms in our Educational Building handicap accessible, not specifically a move to help Beth since she remains in diapers, but which showed how the congregation's sensitivity to the needs of others had grown through the years of having Beth in the family.

***

On May 12 of that year we made what became for several years an annual family pilgrimage to Three Rivers Stadium to watch the Pirates play ball courtesy of the Make a Wish Foundation. Beth had become a Make a Wish Child sometime earlier. (Remember she was not supposed to live past six weeks, six months, three years. By this point she was now ten years old.) The truth about those outings is this: we always got to the festivities late. The Make a Wish folks put on a great pre-game program with some really good food and prizes and activities. The only problem was that we were late for everything. They scheduled them for a Sunday afternoon game that began at 1:35. In case I have failed to mention it or you haven't been paying attention, I am a pastor, one of the folks who only works that hour or two a week in most folks' mind. But that hour is, or was at least for us at the time, 11:00 A.M. on Sunday. So by the time I had greeted the last parishioner and had locked up the building after turning out the lights, we never got off before sometime after 12:30 P.M. With an hour drive to Pittsburgh, we got there as the Make a Wish folks were putting away the last of the food. Truth is Beth hated the game (think loud noises and very crowded walking areas.) But it was our only chance all year to see a game for free, and given our finances at the time, we couldn't afford, or chose not to afford, to actually pay for one.

***

The very next day I took Beth and the girls swimming at the Waynesburg Central High School pool. It is noted here because Beth pooped in the pool. We always put a swim diaper on her before we put her swim suit on. But this time one of us noticed some poop floating in the water and were about to scream a complaint when I realized it was Beth who had done the damage. Try scooping up floating poop while keeping your handicapped kid afloat and trying to discreetly get out of the water as fast as possible. Yikes! You're saying you didn't need to read that, and I am telling you I didn't need to experience it, but it was life with Beth.

***

And then there was the time she nearly died at a local high school basketball game. Merry and I have always had different perceptions of what is best for her in terms of how much freedom we should give her in such places. Merry is more protective and likes to keep a pretty tight rein. I feel like it is good for her to have the freedom to go and come as she chooses. We go to Walmart and I often won't see her for five or ten minutes at a time, something that Merry would be very uncomfortable with.

Well, on this night she was doing her usual thing of driving around the hallways of the school chatting up anyone and everyone who would pay her a little attention. But at some point she had a choke that she was unable to clear. Some folks who were near her came running into the game to get me. When I found her she was slumped over in her chair, eyes shut, pretty out of it. I scooped her up and lay her down on a table in the hallway. I began rigorous percussion therapy and she cleared up quickly. She was soon back in her chair, but not cruising around without her dad close at hand.

***

I have lost track of how many bones Beth has broken through the course of her thirty years but on January 4, 1997 she broke her leg behind and just above her left knee. Somehow she pitched out of her chair. We were at the hospital till 5:00 A.M. The next day at least eight people visited her. Within two days she had received a card in the mail from our good friend Cheri, flowers and a bear from Mrs. Perri, the school librarian, food and balloons from other friends in our church family. And a couple of days later, her teacher at school had brought a Teddy bear with a splint on its leg. The support of our church and school community for Beth has been incredible and remains so even today.

***

CHAPTER THIRTEEN

Mr. Rogers and More 1997-1999

OUR THREE OLDER girls are world travelers. They have all spent weeks, and two of them years abroad. Carrie, our second oldest, spent a year in Norway through the Rotary Club after her senior year in high school. And while she was there, number three daughter, Hannah, visited her while on spring break from school.

If you have ever been to the Pittsburgh airport you know that arriving passengers can exit on one of two sides of the train system that takes them to and from the terminal. It means those waiting for arriving friends or family have to walk back and forth with each arriving train car to see if their loved one has made it. For most of us, it is frankly something of a hassle. For Beth it was, and still is, a total delight to go zooming from one side of the terminal to another in order to be the first one to spot our arriving family member.

That night waiting for Hannah, she must have gone back and forth twenty-five times without growing impatient or otherwise tiring of the effort. Since that night, we don't dare suggest that we arrive in time to have one of the girls just meet us outside at the place where cars can swoop in and pick up arriving passengers. No, we have to be there in plenty of time for Beth to do her thing zooming back and forth.

***

That same spring, she went through a stage where if I forgot to kiss her before leaving or saying good night or whenever she felt it appropriate, she would start saying over and over again, very softly and gently, "Oops." It took me a while at first to catch on to what she was oopsing about, but it became quite endearing once I caught on.

***

On April 10 of that year, we were privileged to visit the set of Mr. Rogers' Neighborhood at the studio of WQED in Pittsburgh where the show originated and was filmed for years on end. Fred Rogers had a special place in his heart for children with disabilities, and so would allow kids like Beth, as well as others from the general population, to be present for the taping of a show.

It was truly a magical time for all of us. We got to visit one on one with Chuck Aber and Lady Aberlin, Miss Paulificate, Larry who did the voice of Prince Tuesday and, of course, Mr. Rogers. Mr. Rogers was running a little late and Beth was getting a bit impatient, so Chuck Aber actually took her out of her chair and held her on his lap for quite some time. Alas, by the time Fred showed up the battery in our old VHS camera with which sister Hannah had been recording the whole thing had died, so we have no video of our time with him.

The man was incredibly gracious, truly the real deal, as sweet and caring as he appears on the show. When filming started, we were escorted to a private viewing room by Mr. Rogers' personal assistant, who stayed with us as long as we remained. Beth seemed to be getting sick so we left not too long after the shooting of the show started.

I was sitting in my office the next morning, when I got a phone call. "Mr. Dorean? This is Fred Rogers." I kid you not. I could have dropped over dead. He explained that he had been hoping to spend more time with us after the show and was sorry that we had not been able to stay. He went on to talk about his friend, Henri Nouwen, the highly respected Christian writer, several of whose books I had read, who had spent years as a personal aide to a severely challenged young man. Mr. Rogers explained that he wanted to send us a book by another friend that detailed his life with a disabled person. We probably talked for ten minutes or so. I was blown away.

***

Two weeks later, while taking her swimming at the high school pool, her chair somehow rolled off the lift of the van and she fell, in the chair, about three feet. Her knees and chin were banged up but incredibly she was otherwise OK. The mercy of God is always amazing, but times like that bring it front and center in a way we cannot help but notice.

***

That Christmas we all went ice skating in Morgantown. One of Carrie's friends from Norway was in to spend the holidays with us, and we had fun forming a human chain holding on to each other, holding on to Beth's chair as she pulled us around the ice. She loved, as always, being the center of attention and being able to serve others.

***

In February of 1998, we began to feel it was time for Beth to understand more about the faith. One night Merry began to explain to her why we love Jesus. "He loves us, He made us. He made me and He made you, Bethany," she said. "And Hannah," Beth added. "Yes, and Hannah too," Merry responded and then continued, "He made plans for us to live

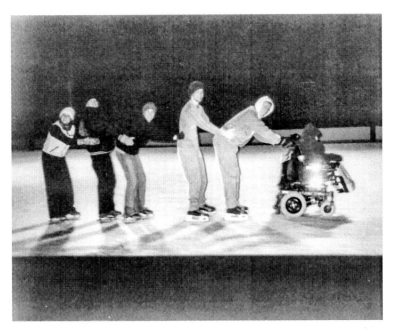

with Him in heaven." "With June," Beth added. (June Scott, a precious friend with whom Beth had a wonderful relationship was probably the first person whose death had impacted her personally.) "Yes, with June," Merry replied.

***

That same month our church began a fund-raising campaign to build an addition on the church parsonage so that Beth could remain on the first floor, without having to be carried up to and down from the second floor for sleeping and bathing. The addition was to include a bathroom with a roll-in shower unit, and her own bedroom. On February 28 we had a pancake breakfast as one of the first parts of that campaign. A thoroughly engaged Beth played her usual role of welcoming every single person who walked in the door.

***

Just a few days later, she began what eighteen years later is still a tradition of joining me when I go to the Jefferson Morgan Elementary school to be one of the volunteer readers for the Read Across America celebration. The school always provides a wonderful luncheon for all of the volunteers prior to our time in the classroom. Beth, being tube fed, cannot enjoy the food, but she more than makes up for that by visiting with all of her "friends."

One year she attached herself to our judge, Farley Toothman, and went everywhere that he went. She was quite disappointed when that same special time with Farley did not work out so nicely the next year, despite the fact that she had talked about another visit with him for weeks ahead of time. Just a month ago I took her to a town hall meeting where folks were speaking about the problem of opiate addiction in our county. Beth was getting tired after nearly two hours and I decided to take her home. She knew she needed to go, but became quite upset when I would not allow her to drive up and greet Farley who was one of the conveners of the gathering.

Merry notes that on May 4 Beth's chair was not working. Emotionally, anything that interferes, even momentarily, to prevent her from being fully in charge of her chair is devastating. I guess it would be like something that incapacitates one of us. She can, right now, go from being sweet and caring, to being mean and snarly when the least thing on her chair needs to be adjusted.

***

The next day, Beth had a very bad choke while Hannah was alone with her. Any choke is wrenching for all of us, but I think Merry and I have a special fear that she will: 1. Choke with someone who will not know how to clear her air passage and/or, 2. Die leaving that person devastated with guilt forever. We have not lived with her all these years without knowing that she could go in an instant (of course, that is true for all of us) so if something like that would happen, we are at least somewhat prepared for it in a way that others might not be. I think we especially hope that it would not happen with one of our daughters, so that they don't spend a minute with regret. Her death is something we all dread, knowing the gaping hole it will leave in all of our lives. Yet we also know the total joy it will bring her to be set free from this body that so limits her joy-filled spirit. Because we get that so clearly, I think Merry and I hope to be a part of that moment and not leave the burden of it to anyone else.

***

As the spring of 1998 progressed, so did the work on the parsonage addition. A series of fund raising events, and a number of generous friends from the community stopping by to write checks, moved the project towards completion with rather remarkable speed. Emily and fiancé, Matt Bonner, had set a date of July 4 for their wedding. In order to be close to Emily and to get to know her family better before the big date, Matt moved in with us for the summer after his graduation from the University of Oklahoma. He worked for the contractor, Tim Phillips, who was doing the work on the addition and got a taste for life doing manual labor before going off to OU Med School in the fall.

The Make A Wish folks provided a spa that we had installed in Beth's new bedroom. Being in water is the only place pressure is off that twisted spine of hers and the heat was soothing to her whole body. We actually got in the spa several times before her room was completed.

A good friend from working with Habitat, Tom McCrae, installed all the plumbing lines to the new bath room, spa and sprinkler system, donating materials as well as his labor. That same thing was true for the tile and new Berber carpet which were donated by one of Beth's favorites, Weaser Humble, from Humble Carpet in Waynesburg. Somehow the sprinkler system went off accidentally the day after the carpet was installed, but no damage was done and we all had a good laugh.

Lonny Walters, our next door neighbor and another one of those jack-of-all-trades that God has blessed our lives with, designed and donated labor and materials to build a railing for the new concrete ramp that was built alongside the addition to facilitate Beth's getting in and out of the house. Our dearest friend Stan Scott worked tirelessly to fashion a special garden area just outside our back door. Matt Bonner shaped a brick edge to that area, and many folks gave of their time and money to make the project a success. In the end, we had more money than we needed and so we began the Bethany Fund that we slowly drew upon over the next fifteen years for special needs that Beth had, like a new lift in the next van we purchased. The love and support of so many people have enriched our lives beyond measure or our ability to properly say thanks.

***

Nowhere has that special bond of love been more formative in her life than through the lives of the men (sorry ladies) who have been such a special part of God's love for Beth through the years. It is hard to make a list of them for fear of leaving one of them out but with special visits (Rodger Foreman used to have "counseling" sessions with Beth), hugs (Lee Goozdich after twenty years still has to give her multiple hugs every time he sees her), conversations (Randy Pettit probably chalked up more talking time with her than anyone), games played with her (Mike Baily certainly racked up the most mileage chasing her after church, though Bill Mundell has been a close second), and phone calls (Dave Calvario and Charlie Anderson may be tied for the most phone calls answering the same questions on every one. What time did you get up this morning? Have you seen Blair this week? Can I call you tomorrow?) Ron Headlee spent quality time with her not only during the years she was at Jefferson-Morgan Elementary, but for years after graduation from high school, he gave up his free period to spend one on one time with her in the gym. And then there are the college age men, Ty Cole, James, Jeremy and Jesse Baker, and still others who have endured Beth's persistent demands for more attention with grace and charm. These men have built Beth's esteem and filled her life with joy in ways we are eternally grateful for.

***

On August 31 of 1998 Beth was back in school for the first day of the year. She was twelve years old and completely thrilled to go off with her Pooh lunch box and a photo of her as the flower girl at her oldest sister's Emily's wedding. Beth had a part in each of her sisters' weddings and was so excited to be in each one.

Beth and Merry and I, but often just Beth and I, would make the three and a half hour drive one way to my sister's about every three months or so. My mom had gone to live in an assisted living place there in Wooster, Ohio, sometime earlier when we deemed it no longer safe for her to be living by herself. Cathy took wonderful care of her, but Beth had had a very special relationship with my mom through the years, and she loved those trips to see Grandma.

It meant my loading her up in the van about 8 A.M., driving for a couple of hours with her in the seat beside me, stopping, lying her down on the back seat, feeding and changing her, driving on to Wooster, getting her back up in her chair, having lunch with Cathy and Grandma, staying till about four and then loading up and doing the whole thing in reverse. We would both get home exhausted, but grateful that we had had that time together and with our Wooster family. Occasionally, Merry would do that same thing, taking Beth to see her other grandparents, and staying a couple days since the drive was twice as long.

***

That fall I continued what became a several year effort to convince the school board to install an elevator in the high school. The Jefferson-Morgan Elementary school was newer, all on one level and completely accessible. But the high school was none of those things. Students in wheelchairs going from any part of the senior high to the cafeteria had to exit the front of the building and walk a couple hundred yards or so around and down a slight incline. That could be an OK experience if the student was in a power chair like Beth's and the weather was nice. Snow or rain and in a manual chair with an aide pushing the chair on icy walks; that was something of a nightmare.

Beth was still years from being in high school (and in fact, in God's providence, never did have any classes in Jefferson Morgan High School itself) It was a particularly tortuous time in school relationships. A recently elected board was bent on not spending a dime of taxpayers' money that did not need to be spent, no matter how worthy the cause. They quickly tired of this persistent pastor raising the issue of what would certainly be a big ticket item of the budget. I ended up taking the side of a superintendent who was hired and then fired three months later for being sympathetic to the teachers' union; several nasty encounters followed that left me all too aware that if an elevator was ever to be built it would not come because of any further efforts of mine. (As it would happen, just a few years after Beth graduated, the president of the board had a child in a wheelchair and the elevator was installed.)

Friday night high school football games also began to become a regular part of the father/daughter relationship that has continued to this day. Her fear of loud noises at first put Beth off from the cheering crowd and the band performances at halftime. But somehow she worked through both. We would go to the games, get through the gate and Beth would be off, driving the sidelines for the next four quarters, chatting up one friend or another. People would stop me and tell me that they had seen her at the other end of the field.

It is another time when Merry would opt for much tighter control, but... She loves the time at home by herself and leaves the two of us to work it out on our own. The whole town knows and loves Beth, so I feel like it is just letting her loose among family, most of whom get a real delight in seeing her cruising along by herself. In recent years, I sometimes make her turn on the lights and four-way flashers that are on her chair, so that I can more easily locate her in the crowd. Of late, we have only been staying till after half time when the band has finished. She once feared the band because of their loudness, but now they are her favorite part of the night. Jon Hildebrand, another of Beth's male favorites and side line attendant at the game, goes back to work then too.

***

In November of 1998, Beth had another incident at school (there are far too many to mention every one) that is worthy of note. For some reason she had a substitute aide. She turned white and the school, thankfully called for the bus that takes her every day, and sent her home. That is what we have requested when she is having difficulty breathing.

It turns out that when she got home, her brace had been put on upside down. Thirty years into putting on the brace multiple times every day, Merry and I still sometimes have to lie her back down because we haven't positioned it well, so it's not like we blame anyone ever for putting it on wrong. But I can only imagine how hard it must have been for her to breathe with that thing constricting her in all the wrong places.

***

A few days later, Beth was outside with Merry putting up some Christmas lights on the ramp that leads into the kitchen. I came to the kitchen door and was standing in it watching the two of them. Beth, still outside, turned to me and said, "Shut that door, I'm cold."

***

I have commented how, for the most part, Beth is blessed by seemingly not being overly aware of the differences between her life and that of others. There is one time every year when she is acutely reminded of those differences. For the thirty-five years we have been at Jefferson, we have led a group of carolers around town, singing to various members of the community. The group varies radically in size, but most often contains a contingent of young kids whose greatest delight is being allowed to run ahead to the next house to ring the doorbell.

Beth desperately wants to join in that activity and asks at almost every house if she can have a turn. Alas, there is not a single home on our route that is accessible for her to get to the door bell, so every year, at every house I am left trying to figure out something she can do that will take the place of ringing the doorbell.

***

In March of 1999, we were at our Monday night prayer gathering, and for some reason some of us had assumed the position of kneeling, not a regular thing in our circles. Not wanting to be left out, speaking of herself as she often does in the third person, Beth said, "Look, Mom, she's on her knees." She was in her chair, bent over leaning her elbows on her knees, a sight I am certain was more pleasing to God than anything the rest of us did that night.

As often happened back in those days, if Beth got any kind of cold, which was an all-the-time happening, nighttimes became particularly dicey. She breathed less deeply and so got even more congested. It always meant her waking up more often trying to clear herself and wanting to be rolled over. On one such night Merry became fearful that the mucous would stop her breathing and so got up and dug out of the pile of old medical equipment we have a manual suction device. By 4:00 A.M. she was exhausted and got me to take over.

The next morning we were scheduled to pick up a new power chair from the Children's Institute, so we whipped over to Children's Hospital where they gave Beth some breathing treatments and gave us the equipment to continue them at home. Just two days later Beth and I went for a quick jog around town, she in the new chair and two days later still we went for a twenty-nine minute jog. Four days after that she was again joining the annual Good Friday Cross Walk from Rices Landing to Jefferson, about five miles in length.

***

On September 29 of 1999 the fragilility of Beth's life smacked us in the face in a very different way than any to date. She and I had gone to a ball game while Merry was at a Ladies' Christian Circle meeting at the church. We were walking home shortly before the game was to end. The sidewalks between the school and the center of town where we live are really bad. (Last year I made an effort to get a grant to replace them, but that is another story for another day.) At one place, they are so heaved up and uneven that

Beth cannot pass so we go out into the road. (You can see where this is going.) We routinely cross at the bottom of a slight grade because it affords us the best view of traffic both directions.

I saw no oncoming cars so said to Beth, "Let's go." We started across. Seemingly out of nowhere, as I had not seen its lights at all, a car came barreling over the top of the rise.

"Stop," I screamed. Beth, frightened by my yelling and not aware of the danger, actually accelerated. "Stop," I screamed again, now lunging for her chair and trying to drag it backwards. Adrenalin can do a lot, but it did not make me Superman. At full acceleration that three hundred and fifty pound chair was not going to be stopped.

Fortunately the driver spotted her in time and came to a screeching stop a few feet from where we both were. I waved and shouted my thanks and we proceeded to go on home. I was shaken to my core at how close we had both come to dying. And, being the idiot that I am, I continued yelling at Beth all the way home. "You've got to listen to your dad when I am speaking to you…" And on I went. We had to get Merry out of her meeting when we got home because we were both so shaken and both felt so awful that we needed some TLC. It would be another five years till she got a new chair, but from that one on, she has had lights and flashers on every chair. That really makes a difference.

***

CHAPTER FOURTEEN

Removing a Lung 2000

T HAT FALL ALSO began a pattern of Beth's health that would end in a desperate effort to make some change in her condition. She had been sick on and off since birth. But that September, as she returned to school, began an endless routine of sickness, being home for a week to get well, returning to school for a day or two, before getting sick again, being home for a week and on and on. We tried sending her for only half a day to keep her strength up and to make sure her getting sick was not from being overly fatigued. We tried sending her every other day, all to no avail.

I began pounding her (percussion therapy) every time she would wake me at night. Instead of the quick roll her over and get her and me back to sleep as quickly as possible, I would get out of bed and do ten or fifteen minutes of percussion therapy. It definitely made a difference in how she made it through the nights, though little if any difference in terms of her staying well.

In late November, she got pneumonia still again and was put on two hard core antibiotics that were really hard on her.

I have mentioned our near reverence for Dr. Zitelli. Well, think about this. During the time that she was on those antibiotics, Dr. Z called us twice to check up on her. The doctor calling the patient? Really? No, "Hey give me a call and I'll put you on hold for half an hour." No, "Give my office a call to let us know how things are working out." No, he called us.

Recovered for a few days, Beth made her favorite trip to the airport to pick up her favorite person, sister Hannah, who had been off in GA for the fall working with a Christian community, Jubilee Partners, that focuses on refugee resettlement. Beth was so happy to see Hannah and kept stopping, as we were trying to get to our car, to give her one more hug.

***

January 2000 was a month of balloon ball in the Dorean household. We had begun the practice years ago. Beth, lying on her gurney, would swat at a passing balloon and those playing with her would work to keep it aloft. The rules varied as much as those playing, but the game kept her rolling from side to side and seemed more effective than percussion therapy in keeping her clear. No one who entered the house, strangers or lifelong friends, got a bye from playing. So whatever your preference for or against, get over it and get into the game.

***

For all of our efforts, Beth kept getting sick again and again. One choir practice she got so chokey that we had to put her down on the floor where she remained quite content for about half an hour. If you think that is cold or unhealthy or inappropriate, welcome to our world. We felt like we were in a constant battle of trying to keep her well and at the same time keeping her involved with as much of the normal routines of life as possible. Taking her home on an occasion like this was, of course, an option, but it meant further isolation for her and one of us, something of which there was already too much of.

As we moved into February, she had one bad choke after another. One time in school she actually lost consciousness momentarily. Another one occurred just days later when she and Merry were at the post office, a block from our home. Merry called me, I drove down, Merry drove Beth home lying down in the van and I sat in the chair and drove it home.

***

A moment of lightness occurred when Carrie and her friend Jen arrived home for spring break from Wheaton. They arrived at 2:30 A.M. and Beth woke up when they came in the door. We spent some time laughing and hugging in the dark before everyone went to bed. In the morning, we woke up the sleepy heads by putting Beth in bed with Carrie. That remains one of Beth's all-time favorite ways of "tricking" folks.

***

On March 15, she had a bad choke on the school bus, and they had to stop and lie her down on the floor till she cleared. Now that was a dirty floor, but again the alternative, to keep her forever at home, seemed even less desirable.

Several trips to Children's took place, with x-rays, a salivagram, echocardiogram, blood gases and a multitude of other tests taking place. Hannah spent most of one day lying on a variety of tables beside Beth to keep her still or entertained during the tests. Hannah was herself exhausted at the end of the day, so one can only imagine how the kid who was already weak and sick to start with was feeling.

On April 24 Beth and I left for Children's at 5:00A.M. for a lung CAT scan. But there was a scheduling error so we ended up waiting a long time. They had been fearful that they might have to sedate her for the scan, and no one wanted to sedate her ever for anything for fear she wouldn't come out of it. But it was an open scan and I was able to keep my head very close to hers and kept talking and encouraging her to lie still and they were able to complete the scan without anything to quiet her. Praise God.

We had had a broncoscopy scheduled so that they could get a clearer picture of what was going on in that partially collapsed left lung, but by May 4, after days of fever and chokiness, we just had to go to the hospital a day early. We were several nights in a row up all night pounding her with little to no improvement.

The broncoscopy showed that her left lung was full of infection. But the right lung was really surprisingly good and had actually grown in size as it filled the expanding cavity caused by the twisting of the spine that was crushing the left lung. It was succeeding in compensating for the failing left one, to some extent at least. So the bevy of specialists working with Beth began to talk seriously for the first time about the possibility of removing the left lung.

It quickly became a now or never decision, because it seemed like her condition would only continue to decline. And the weaker she got, the less chance of pulling through the surgery there was. So we all agreed to proceed.

Two days before the surgery was to take place, Beth began
to scream as if in horrific pain. We thought she had developed
a mucous plug that had collapsed one or the other lung, but
it turned out to be pulmonary embolisms. Had we not been
at Children's she would almost certainly have died. As it was,
she was put on blood thinners and moved to ICU.

In the midst of all of this, the normal processes of child
maturity continued, if a bit delayed. Beth lost a tooth and then
a second while in ICU. Phone calls with her sisters not in
town were a daily happening and visits from friends and the
whole church community were the order of the day.

Beth made friends with everyone she met, begged hugs
from anyone and everyone who looked like they might be
vulnerable to her asking.

She remembered, and still does, names of new faces far
better than any of the rest of us. She loved answering the
phone beside her bed or one of our cell phones. "I'll get it,"
she would say every time a phone rang. "Hello, Bethany's
room."

She connived one of the nurses into playing Old Maid with
her and charmed the nurses and doctors every bit as much as
the rest of us. Once when Merry was having a very serious
conversation with Dr. Zitelli about her future, Beth
interrupted, "Please be a little quiet. I am talking to Rodger."
Sister Hannah spent a night sleeping at the foot of Beth's bed
and that night our sicky slept eleven hours with hardly a stir.

The surgery was moved to May 10. The day before, her
room was flooded with balloons and cards seemingly from
every corner of the globe. Emily flew in from OK. Shortly
after she arrived at the hospital, Beth grabbed a flashlight we
had been using to maneuver around the room when the lights

were off so as not to wake her. Shining the light she announced, "I'm telling a story. Long ago in a far away land a princess got married. I'm picking the princess, my sweetheart Hannah. I'm picking the mother, Mom. I'm picking the prince, Carrie. I'm picking the fairy godmother, Dad. The frog is Emily. That's it. Story's over. The End."

The surgery kept getting put off, as the doctors were making sure that the embolisms were gone. It finally occurred on May 16. Three men from the church spent most of the day with us. Carrie, who had flown in from France for the surgery, ended up having to take Hannah to the airport to fly to CO before the surgery was completed. Han was already a week late to start training to be a white water rafting guide at Noah's Ark.

As it turned out, the lung came out pretty easily and Beth did remarkably well. Her breathing tube was removed less than twenty-four hours later. Merry, Carrie and I were staying at the nearby Ronald McDonald House and taking turns being with her round the clock. Merry's sisters, Louise and Jane, arrived and had a good time laughing it up with Beth. The second day two IVs and her catheter were removed and all seemed to be doing great.

She was incredibly thirsty from the twenty-four hours on the ventilator and her throat was no doubt a little sore. She begged to be able to sip water off of one of those little foam sponges on a stick that they give you to dab out your mouth when you aren't allowed to drink. We were all amazed at how well she seemed to be handling it all, until she got suddenly desperately chokey. It turned out all the water had been going directly into her lung. So she had to be immediately intubated. That was emotionally very hard for all of us.

A day later, while Merry was sitting in the surgical waiting area, a nurse came to get her. Beth had extubated the tube with her tongue. I had heard of folks pulling the tube out, but never like that. But she was doing fine and proceeded to make improvements. That night, having done a wedding rehearsal at 7:00P.M., it was my night to be by her side in ICU, so I did the wedding the next day without sleep. It seems crazy looking back at it, but that was just part of the way life rolled at the time.

By May 22 she was off oxygen completely, her dressing was removed, her SAT levels (that measure the oxygen saturation levels in blood) when sitting up were good, so Dr. Zitelli announced it was time for her to get up in her chair. She rode around for ten minutes. The old spark was returning.

She had several nights of really good sleep, increased her time in the chair to thirty minutes twice a day and, on May 26, she came home.

We got oxygen tanks and an oxygen concentrator for her to be on at night and a pulse ox machine to monitor her levels throughout the night and day.

On May 28, Beth drove to the front of the church, took the microphone in her hand (she is such a ham) and said, "Thanks for praying for me, guys."

***

On June 1 it was time to take Carrie to the airport. Being a photographer before the age of digital cameras, she had a lot of film with her that she did not want to go through an x-ray machine at security so she/we were there quite a while getting that all worked out. Meanwhile, Beth was zooming around the airport at full speed bringing smiles to folks who seemed delighted to be watching her go.

***

By August 10, we were off to the Philadelphia area to visit Merry's family. One night we all went to have a picnic at Washington's Crossing and to watch an outdoor production of the Sound of Music. Beth loved it. The production has been a family favorite for years. Even as I am typing this, literally, we are watching it for the I-can't-begin-to-guess-how-many times. Beth knows most all of the songs by heart and loves to sing them at the top of her voice. She is especially happy if she can entice me into singing along with her. But this show was special because we got to do it with a large number of Merry's family. (Read from Beth's perspective: so many people for me to get attention from.) The "stage" was kind of carved out of a hill side, but the viewing area was very accessible. She loved tooling around and chatting everyone up. And the outdoor environment meant she could sing along without being a distraction.

***

For all of her struggles that most of us never face, Beth was also not immune from the kind of accidents that just sort of happen. A good friend was learning to feed and change Beth. (A lot of folks are just too afraid of her delicate state to even try something as simple as that.) She had Beth on the floor, and while she was busy attending to Beth, her own little daughter climbed into Beth's chair and proceeded to back into Beth's head. Tire marks were imprinted on her head and remained for several days, leaving Merry understandably clingy towards her.

But a couple of weeks later, those two indomitable spirits were out working together in the garden, Merry digging holes, and Beth dropping from long range tulip bulbs into the holes.

Then on October 24, we drove south to Jubilee Partners, a Christian community working on refugee resettlement and an offshoot of Koinonia. I was leading three sessions of their yearly retreat. Jubilee is a beautiful spot, but with their emphasis on simple living, they had only dirt paths between buildings and a lot of open ground. Normally rough terrain like that is a real downer for Beth who much prefers nice smooth pavement. But after a day or so she began to get used to the rougher ground and actually began to enjoy careening all over the place at a high rate of speed. A good friend and resident partner at Jubilee, Don Mosley, convinced Beth to let him try out her chair on one occasion, and she, like all of the rest of us, had a good laugh at watching him trying to drive it around, bouncing hither and yon, with none of her giftedness.

***

The last day of this momentous year was in many ways the culmination of her life to that point. That morning, as a part of our regular worship service at Jefferson Baptist, she was baptized. For those of you not familiar with Baptist tradition, that means she was immersed, dunked. We give folks a chance to give their testimony, if they like. Most decline, but Merry convinced Beth to memorize the 23rd Psalm which she recited, with quite a bit of help from sister Hannah, who, along with the rest of the family, were in for the holidays. Brother-in-law Matt lifted her out of her chair and lowered her to me. And then, long time friend and deacon, Pete Arigoni, joined me in lowering her into the water. She did great and our church family rejoiced again in the goodness of God.

***

The next Sunday, Beth was taken into membership in our church. The youth group was going again for their annual trip to BOPARK in Morgantown to go ice-skating. Beth remembered the fun that she had had and very much wanted to go again. I confess that I was just too tired and so did not take her. I fear that that scenario has gotten played out again and again in her life. Because she is so dependent on someone else, most often her parents, to get her where she needs to or wants to be, she must rely on their/our willingness to take her. A lot of the time we are just too fried to pull off what she wants to do. It makes us all quite sad.

***

CHAPTER FIFTEEN

Fighting for Life Again 2002-2003

THE SUMMER OF 2001 Beth began going to a special ed class at Margaret Bell Miller Middle School in Waynesburg with Dennis Mattei as her instructor. Dennis was a remarkable guy, a former body builder and aerobics teacher. Merry had worked out with a class of ladies he led years earlier. He had a love and understanding for kids with disabilities unlike anything I have ever seen in someone else. He and Beth hit it off right away, and he nurtured her in and out of the classroom for many years to come.

Dennis' class went to the high school pool for their physical education class once a week. Because there was not enough staff to keep all of the kids safely afloat, I went with Beth each Wednesday morning. It was always a special time. While I, of necessity, concentrated my focus and energy on Beth, there was always the need to help with some other child. It was another one of those experiences where I got so much more out of it than I gave.

***

At the beginning of 2002, Merry and I had a once in a lifetime opportunity to go to Australia. A young woman in our congregation, Emily Wigington Johnson, was getting married there to a young man, Kable Dale, she had met while

doing a stint with the Rotary in Hungary. She asked her mom, Linda, to have me do the wedding. In an incredibly generous offer, Linda paid for both Merry and me to fly to Australia, put us up in a very nice motel and provided most of our meals. It was one of the most special times of our married years.

It was only possible because our daughters, Emily and Hannah, tag teamed Beth's care. Em was living in Pittsburgh where Matt was doing his residency in ER medicine at UPMC and Hannah lived at home.

Emily was pregnant with our first grandchild, Asa, and got quite sick. Not wanting to go to school one morning, Beth faked illness as she was quite adept at doing, saying that she was, "Throwing up like Emily." Hearing her story and not buying it for a minute, the girls explained in a note to Dennis about the situation at home, so he would be aware of her attempt to get a free pass on doing anything at school because of illness. He wrote back, "Thanks, but we are already on to Bethany."

A snow day a week later had the girls telling Beth that she had a two hour delay. In her sometimes imperfect speech that phrase became for years, a "duour duway."

We were gone to Australia for twelve days and because Em was so sick, the brunt of the load fell on Hannah. We called almost every day we were gone. Working out the time difference so that we could talk with them meant that we had to wake up early to catch them before they went to bed at night. But in those calls, we could hear the weariness growing in Hannah as the days went by. Amazingly, when we returned she did not say, "Never again," and, in fact, has performed similar gifts of letting us go away numerous times. though never again for such a long period of time.

***

On February 5, our good friend and family doctor, Martha Noftzger, brought by a Jack Russell terrier named Lucy for us to try out as a companion dog for Beth. Martha's mom had been a vet and she herself has made a huge commitment of time and resources to our local humane society, so is always bringing home another rescue animal. Lucy had, we discovered sometime later, actually been the dog of some friends of ours, but had gotten away while they were dealing with their own medical crises. She was timid and shy and not yappy like a lot of Jack Russells. Martha hoped she might cuddle with Beth and be a real source of delight for her. That never quite worked out, but the family enjoyed our many years with her.

***

On April 9, Merry made one of the best phone calls of our family's life. Beth had gone through a series of aides that school year that just didn't work out well, for one reason or another. And she was getting quite frustrated with the situation. Her aide spent as much time during the day with her as we had with her while she was home, so it seemed really essential that we get someone with whom she got along well. We had been blessed by a number of wonderful ladies who cared for her while she was at Jefferson Morgan Elementary, notably Katrina Collins, but the transition of schools for some reason caused problems.

Merry called Billie Jo Balazick, a friend from church, who over the next years became another member of the family. She had a feel for what Beth was thinking and feeling and had the ability to call her bluff when she was faking, as well as bring her the most tender care when she needed it. What a total blessing she was for the rest of Beth's time in school, and remains even now all these years later. On a recent trip to CO for the birth of our ninth grandchild, Beth called Billie every day, asking almost exactly the same questions each day, and getting kind, patient and informative answers to each one. What a blessing!

***

That summer, it was the turn of daughter number two, Carrie, to be in town for the summer, making plans for an August wedding. Her fiancé, Ryan Hobert, was staying with us for the summer, as Matt Bonner had done before marrying Emily. Ryan worked with the County and at a local greenhouse. Carrie volunteered to take over for Billie so that Billie could be home with her own kids. It worked well for everyone, as Carrie needed the money and Billie was glad for the break.

That fall we made another trip to Wildwood, NJ, courtesy of Paul and Joan Ankney. Paul and his mom and sister had gone to church at JBC and his dad and I had played together on the church softball team. I had the sorrowful privilege of doing Paul Sr.'s funeral when he was killed tragically in a coal mining accident. Paul Jr. and Joan for several years made a rental house next to theirs available to our family after the summer rush was over. Beth loved the wide boardwalk and swimming in the pool in the backyard. We loved being near beautiful Cape May, just a few minutes' drive away.

Several times that week we rented a two person trike to ride on the boardwalk, taking turns pedaling Beth up and down the streets. She loved it. When we got home, Merry looked into buying one, and before long we were pedaling our two person trike around town, and with the help of Parks and Rec director, Jake Blaker, on the Greene River Trail. A couple of months after we got the trike, Mr. Mattei agreed to let us bring it to school, and his entire class had the thrill of riding around the enclosed playground on it, accompanied by someone with the ability to pedal and steer it. It was never the big hit for Beth here in Greene County that it was in Wildwood, but church kids and now grandkids love jumping up and spinning around the neighborhood on it.

***

At Christmastime that year, Beth offered to let Matt and Emily go to a movie while she watched six-month-old Asa. We laugh at it because caring for a baby is so totally beyond her physical abilities. Yet her intentions are the best and I am not really sure she understands that she cannot do it, another example of her just not being conscious of her many limitations. Praise God.

***

January 19, 2003 began what may well have been the most difficult twenty-three days of any of our lives. As the new year began, Beth was once again sick, frequently. Under the supervision of her doctors, we pulled out every one of the techniques that had worked in the past: oxygen, antibiotics, Albuterol, Tylenol, Ibuprofen, percussion therapy, all to no avail. On the nineteenth, we actually called for the Jefferson Ambulance and they graciously took her to Children's.

We had not been there long before several conferences with doctors began. The general consensus of the team of doctors working with her, led by Dr. Zitelli and including pulmonary and ICU specialists, was that Beth had pneumonia and was nearing the end of her time here on earth. We sobbed as they described what they believed would be a continuing downward spiral as the muscle weakness that had been her enemy since birth persistently inhibited her pulmonary functions.

One of the team of ICU specialists who were working with her on a daily, hour by hour basis was of the opinion that we should let them do a tracheotomy on her to enable her to have greater ease in breathing and to enable us to assist in providing her with a clear airway. He spoke of kids whom he had performed the surgery on who lived relatively healthy lives for years on end.

Our concern was, of course, quality of life. Beth is such a talker, and gains so much joy from any conversation directed her way. It felt to us like we would be removing one of the very few pleasures in her life, so we resisted his fairly strong pressure to do it.

Personally, I felt that they were likely correct about this being the end. Though she had been relatively healthy since the removal of the lung, her condition was so fragile, and we seemed unable, even at the miracle working Children's, to get on top of this recent slew of infections.

The concern I expressed was that she not suffer. As a pastor, I have been with too many folks at the end of life who died gasping for breath, something obviously painful for them, but heart-wrenching as well for their families to endure. Basil and others assured us that they would be able to keep Beth comfortable with the use of morphine and other drugs that would ease her out of this life.

So we prepared to say goodbye. We signed a Do Not Resuscitate order and told the girls what we thought was happening. Carrie flew in the next day from France, followed several days later by Ryan, and Hannah came home from Dickinson College. Emily and Asa were with us all the time as they lived only minutes from the hospital and Matt came as often as his residency allowed.

Just a day or two after the DNR order had been signed, Beth developed a huge mucous plug and coded (stopped breathing). Her numbers plummeted and we thought this was it. Billie Jo Balazick and great friend, Stan Scott, were visiting at the time, and Billie held me as I sobbed at the end of her bed. Merry was right beside Beth and a team of doctors and nurses from the ICU descended upon her, bagging her until she cleared and could resume breathing on her own. Weeping now with joy, we asked why they had not followed the DNR. And they explained that as ICU specialists their responsibility was to do everything in their power to save life, so that's what they had done. They would, in effect, only follow a DNR if they deemed that they would be unable to restore life. We were certainly grateful that they knew better than us the parameters of these life and death issues.

Having been brought back from near death, Beth's condition stabilized. But now she battled something almost as threatening as the physical illness. The ICU at Children's at the time was one big room, only a small corner of which ever got any daylight from windows high up the wall. So day in and day out, though the staff did their best to let nighttime be nighttime, significantly darkening the room, lights shone on in an endless fashion. Beth, like other long term patients in the unit, developed what is called ICU syndrome. It is like they develop a disconnect between what is going on in their life and reality. Countless visitors, including Merry's sisters, Jane and Louise, and my sister, Cathy, some of her favorite men, and virtually every friend we have in the world, visited, but none were able to break through this trance-like state she had slipped into. We couldn't kid her into laughing or even smiling. It was almost like she was in a drugged state. In the midst of this particularly bleak time, Hannah had to return to college, an emotional blow for all of us but, most of all, for Beth.

After more than two weeks, a bed opened nearer the natural light portion of the room and we swooped in to grab it. Even that made little difference.

But someone, I am not sure who it was, suggested that we try a bipap machine to facilitate her breathing by helping to keep her lung clear. Unlike the C-pap that is used by many folks who suffer with sleep apnea, the bi-pap both blows air into the lungs and sucks it back out. Initially it is more uncomfortable, though Beth struggled very little with it. She responded well, and it really seemed to be a major help in drawing out of her the mucous that was pooling in her lung from her inability to breathe deeply. For the first several weeks she was on it twenty-four hours a day. And she cleared up.

The physical danger was past and it was time to go home. She remained lethargic, unresponsive to our efforts to cheer her up. Great friend after great friend visited, all assuring her that soon she would be going home. No response.

Finally the day came. Our faithful crew from the Jefferson Ambulance Service returned to Children's to pick her up. Still no response as they took her from the ICU and loaded her in the ambulance. Merry was the designated parent to ride along with her, while I stayed behind to gather up all of our stuff accumulated through twenty-three days in the ICU and the equipment which we were taking home with us.

On the hour long drive home, Merry kept telling Beth they were driving home, to stay. Beth didn't seem to care. But as she began to see some landmarks she recognized on the drive she had traveled so many times before, she began to show more interest. Beth looked up at her Mom riding beside her and said, "I'm going home." By the time I got home, she was like a new kid from the one that had left the hospital. She was her usual self, taking phone calls, while directing visitors to the home to wait while she took a call. "Miss I-am-in-Control" was back.

***

A few days after she got home, Merry and I had a long talk with Jon Coote, our good friend and master woodworker. We had been so close to death and realized that there was much we did not have in order if such an event occurred. So we had a tearful conversation with Jon about building a casket for Beth. Friends we had known in Georgia had had their caskets built while they were in their twenties and have used them all of their lives as chests for blankets and such. That was what we imagined here. We talked and talked and it was all a bit much for Jon emotionally. He assured us that he would take care of it, and the subject has never been broached since.

***

A day after that conversation, Fred Rogers died. He had come to feel like part of our family and his death to pancreatic cancer saddened us all. Our neighborhood would never be quite the same again, though to this day we watch episodes on YouTube. Carrie had returned to France a few days prior and the whole Dorean house was in a low state for quite some time. Carrie had put her heart into lifting Beth's spirits, with balloon ball, exercise sessions and tea parties. We sure missed her brightness when she was gone.

Emily Dale was stuck stateside for a number of months, apart from her Australian husband due to visa issues. She graciously volunteered many hours doing many of the same cheering services for Beth. And Billie Jo came almost every day for the next month, as the school allowed her to serve as an educational aide. Her cheerfulness eventually carried the day and lifted all of our spirits. On March 24, more than two months after her last day there, Beth finally returned to school with Mr. Mattei and her classmates. Dennis had visited her several times at home and made it clear that she had better not keep the class waiting much longer. What a party the day she entered that classroom!

For that last five weeks or so that she was recuperating at home, Beth spent most of her days and nights in a hospital bed that we parked beside the big front window in our living room. She was the center of our life and liked watching all that was going on outside, whether it was dad shoveling or mom walking to the post office or folks coming and going from church. On March 31, we removed the hospital bed from the house. It's never been back!

***

Not until May 14, almost four months after she was admitted to Children's, did her pulmonologist give us permission to begin slowly weaning her from twenty-four hour a day oxygen use. She had had to come off of the bipap when she began getting up in her chair for short periods of time and tolerated that well, but we had continued with the oxygen. We began with removing her just fifteen minutes at a time. But she did well and was, before too long, off it completely except for naps and bedtime when she was also on the bipap.

***

It was always difficult to stay up with all that needed to get done at home, at work, with the family and community. It would be May 22 before Merry, God bless her, finished writing the last of the "thank yous" that she wrote for gifts and cards and visits from that hospitalization that began in January. I am sure no one would have held it against us if they never got such a card, but Merry has always tried to be diligent about letting folks know we appreciate their kindness.

***

CHAPTER SIXTEEN

Legally An Adult 2004

JULY 4 OF 2003 was also a notable day for us. Beth had never wanted to watch the town's fireworks because of the pain of loud noises, so would often retreat inside the house when they began. The front lawn of our church has a great view of them, so we began many years ago having a party on the fourth with Bocce Ball and food and games of Trivial Pursuit and the like. We often had thirty or forty folks join us for the evening, which Beth would enjoy till the first firework went off.

This year was different because she made it through the first round and, by then, good friends, Mark Perry and Mike Dohanich, were entertaining us all with their oohs and ahs and, "I liked that one." They were so goofy that Beth forgot about the noise and joined in with their banter. Since that day she looks forward to the fireworks and though she occasionally will make whining sounds about going inside before they start, when the action begins, she is out there on the lawn going, "I liked that one," even though neither of those two men still joins us.

***

The winter of 2004 saw Beth experience two accidents that seemed close to catastrophic at the time, but turned out to be no big deal. Dressing her for winter was always a challenge, getting a coat that would fit over her brace and not be too restrictive in her chair. We had what we thought was the perfect option in a beautiful wool poncho that we could put on after she was in the chair and that provided some all body warmth. But then one day a portion of the poncho got caught in her wheel and pulled her head down with a jerk. Not realizing what was happening she held her hand on the joy stick only increasing the pressure on her neck. We were not close at hand, so someone from the church had to come get us. Obviously, the second we saw what was happening, we jumped in and backed her chair up, releasing the pressure. She seemed OK but phoosh! That was a scary moment.

Just two weeks later Merry got a rare opportunity to join Ryan, Carrie, Emily and Matt for ten days or so in France. Carrie and Ryan were living there at the time while he went to graduate school in Paris (his parents have been missionaries there for thirty-five years), and the others were visiting them. Hannah kept Merry's "Beth journal" going while she was away and noted a time when Beth fell and hit her head hard. Again she seemed all right, but Hannah describes her milking the fall for all it was worth, calling friends and family members like there was no tomorrow.

***

We found out that summer that Beth had become too old to continue in Mr. Mattei's Middle School class. We checked out options at Waynesburg Central and Jefferson Morgan.

WCHS's classroom was impossibly small for her to manage her chair in. And attending Jefferson Morgan would have meant that she would be mainstreamed in regular classes with an aide to assist her.

We settled on a newly formed program beginning at the old East Franklin Elementary school in Waynesburg. It had classes for special needs kids like Beth, and for students who had had disciplinary issues in their regular schools. The building had a ton of space, and with Billie Jo by her side, we were reasonably confident all would be OK. We gave it a try, but a couple of weeks into her time there, Billie made clear that she didn't think it was a good situation for Beth. At that point, at Mr. Mattei's suggestion, we wrote a letter asking for a special exemption so that she would be able to finish out her years of eligibility to attend public school in his classroom. It is a measure of Beth's child-like nature and looks, and a testament to Dennis and those who worked with him, that it remained a good place for her till she was twenty-one. We will be forever grateful to the folks at Margaret Bell Miller for allowing that arrangement.

***

When Beth turned eighteen that July, we, as her parents, were no longer allowed access to her medical records or to act on her behalf. It was one of those kind of ridiculous things, a good regulation but one totally unsuitable for Beth's situation. It is not like she could give anyone an intelligible decision about her care.

Anyway, it required us to go to court to apply for guardianship of our own daughter. The process was not just a matter of signing a few papers. A neutral party had to explain guardianship to Beth and gain her consent to have us become her guardians, as well as being mom and dad. Once again, Dennis Mattei came through for us. So they met in the office of Kathy Davis, who directed this entire effort and, with incredible generosity, donated her time in preparing all of the legal documents that were required.

On December 13, 2004, the three of us appeared before Greene County Judge Bill Nalitz for our guardianship hearing. The always competent Kathy again directed us through that time. Merry and I testified (Beth desperately wanted to as well but nobody asked her to do so.) Dennis appeared and testified in a very flattering way about our role as her parents. We not only got approved, but Judge Nalitz also waived most of the court fees.

***

2004 ended, as most years at this season of our lives did, with Merry and I hosting anyone from the church family who wanted to come on New Year's Eve for a fifteen minute time of prayer and communion. It was an intimate time of sharing. Folks would come into the candlelit sanctuary, tell us what was going on in their lives, and we would pray for them and serve them communion. When we first began the practice, we did it for a couple of hours after supper on New Year's Eve. The time became so special in the life of the church that that year we began meeting with people at 1:00 in the afternoon and didn't finish up till after 9:00 in the evening, with maybe half an hour out for a quick supper.

We would always come home drained yet thrilled with the joy of all that time with such wonderful folks. I mention that because of the care that Beth in turn received while we were busy next door. Billie Jo's daughter, Leah, watched her most of the afternoon, Brittany Blair-Martin did a turn in the

168

evening and Beth's telephone buddies, Albert and Norma Starostanko, took over and stayed until we got home. What might otherwise have been a long and boring day for her, instead became a wonderful occasion because of the caring spirit of these great folks.

***

On March 30 of 2005, Merry, Beth and I drove to the Outer Banks for a few days with the family of Merry's sister, Louise. Her husband, Bob, the best natural athlete I have ever met, had just been diagnosed with ALS and some good friends of theirs had loaned them an incredibly large and beautiful house right on the beach for a month to six weeks so that they could process what lay ahead of them with their large network of friends and family.

For those who have never been to the Outer Banks, this was a section where the only way to the house where they were staying was to drive up the beach. The house could only be accessed at low tide, and even then, only with a four-wheel drive vehicle. That meant we had to park not only our van, but Beth's wheelchair, at a site off the beach and have one of the family drive us to the house. So Beth was very restricted in movement the days we were there. But the whole experience was quite remarkable for all of us.

Bob was not yet in a wheelchair, but was very definitely already in the throes of limited mobility and difficult breathing. Watching this incredibly fit man struggle with his own motor neuron related disease was emotionally difficult but at the same time enlightening. While his ALS was an ever worsening disease, and hers static, it gave me an ever greater respect for the enormous strength of our girl who had battled against similar muscle weakness her whole life. One can only imagine what kind of incredible athlete she might have been had she not had to combat such a crippling disease.

***

Something of that rugged, never-give-up spirit was evident a few weeks later in what has become something of a regular happening around here. I had visited friends and church members, Barry and Maria Guesman, at the birth of their second son Aiden at Ruby Memorial Hospital in Morgantown. On the way home I had stopped in at Waynesburg Central for a swim. I didn't get home till it was dark and nearly 8:30 at night. There in the headlight of my car, as I pulled into our parking lot, was my faithful daughter sitting alone in her chair, waiting for dad to come home. She had been there for almost two hours, refusing her mother's entreaties to come in, sure that dad would call before he got home to let her know he was on the way. Oops!

***

Later that year, Beth delivered one of her classic lines that she brings forth every now and then. You really have to know the show it is taken from and the riotous laughter it brings forth from our family to truly appreciate this story but... For years now one of our all time family favorite TV shows has been "The Lucy Show" where Lucy becomes a spokesperson for Vita Veta Vegamin, one of those products guaranteed to do anything and everything you could ever want it to do for you. The advertisement Lucy is doing for the product begins, "Friends, are you tired, run down, listless? Do you poop out at parties?" We howl when we watch it. One night, Beth was having a particularly restless sleep, waking me up way too often. And I finally complained. "Beth, you've gotta let me get some sleep." And from nowhere (this is about 4:00 A.M.) comes this voice, "Are you tired, run down, listless? Do you poop out at parties?" How could I do anything but laugh!

And speaking of laughing, one of Beth's all-time favorite pastimes is to lie on the bed with Hannah or Carrie, and laugh.

Actually, the game goes something like this. "Hannah, laugh like Mom." And Hannah will do her best (and she is pretty good at it) to laugh in the distinctive style of Merry. "Laugh like Carrie…" And on they go through the whole family and anyone else that they can think of who has a distinctive laugh. It is a hoot to watch them together. Beth has her own belly laugh or sometimes laughs so hard she can barely catch her breath.

***

Another family routine is the nightly bed race. Most nights we get Beth ready for bed (feeding her, washing her face and hands and button spot, putting on a t-shirt for sleeping in, changing her diapers, brushing and cleaning her teeth with gauze) in the living room, while she is lying on her gurney watching TV. Whoever is getting her ready kind of slyly waits till the other has left the room or is focused elsewhere and then scoops Beth up or pushes her gurney into her bedroom.

Most often that move has been sniffed out well in advance and there is a race to the bed. Technically, (at least, according to Dad's rules) winning involves getting Beth to bed and lying beside her before anyone else gets there. When the grandkids are in town, it's pretty much whoever gets there before Grandpa and Beth is the winner. We have been known to bang Beth's feet or head off the doorway racing to get to the bed first, which only adds to Beth convulsing in laughter. She is crushed when no one is around or, worse yet, no one has the energy to do it. I will often scoop her up in my arms, say in a whispered voice, "Shh," and run with her to the bed, throwing us both down on it. "We sure crushed those guys!" And Beth will hold up her version of the loser sign with her two crooked fingers, howling with laughter.

***

CHAPTER SEVENTEEN

Graduation Days 2006 Thru 2008

IN MARCH OF 2006, I made a trip, along with other American Baptists from southwestern PA, to Bluefields, Nicaragua, where it just so happened Hannah was finishing up a seven month internship with Ketly and Vital Pierre. Hannah was the only one of the three girls who had not done a semester or more abroad while in college, but she sure made up for it in the years after graduation. It was a total delight to spend eight or nine days working side-by-side with her and the others from western PA, including four from Jefferson Baptist, and our new Nicaraguan friends.

What became so apparent during that trip was how essential it was for Beth to be in regular contact with us when we were gone. Though only ten years ago, this was before the time of the now ubiquitous cell phone that could easily handle calls from all over the globe. Phone service in this second poorest nation in the world was extremely limited, so Hannah and I would have to go into town to the precursor of an internet café and use one of the dozens of phones they had available for folks like us to use to call the States.

I confess that left to myself I would have been much more casual about getting the call made, but Hannah realized just how important it would be to Beth that we touch base daily. So when work was done and showers finished, while everyone else was stretching out to relax, she and I were walking the mile to a place we could catch a sketchy taxi for the ride into town to make our phone call. Merry told us later how Beth would do nothing else (like get ready for bed) till she had had her call from Nicaragua.

***

A few weeks after we returned, the four of us went to Waynesburg University to see Ken Medema in concert. For those not familiar with Ken, he is a blind Christian musician who sings and plays the piano, a remarkably talented man. Merry and I had had the privilege of hearing him in concert several times previously, but this was Beth's first chance. She loved it, loved his music, but also loved meeting him personally after the concert. The two of them, each with their very different disabilities, just clicked. Ken is the kind of guy who is kind and sympathetic to any and all, but you could see his whole countenance fill with an even greater joy in the few minutes they spent together. Seeing them bonding was like a foretaste of heaven.

***

That spring Merry took Beth to Walmart to purchase a new pair of sandals. Every now and then we have to buy her new shoes just for a change of pace since hers never wear out. Finding a pair that suited them both, Beth asked Merry, "Can I take a walk in them?" Once again, she just doesn't quite get the difference between her and us in taking a walk. But it is a beautiful thing.

***

On May 23, 2006 our first granddaughter, Samara, was born. We had gone to OK to welcome the new grandchild into the world, but Emily was late in delivering her. We three loved playing with her two older brothers, Asa and Phin, who were four and two at the time. The day before we were to leave for home, Em went into labor. We decided to leave Merry with the Bonners to help with the new baby, and Beth and I drove home alone, stopping at the hospital to see the precious newborn on our way out of town.

She and I had a great time on that trip home. She would sit up front with me for hours at a time and when her back gave out, I would lie her down in the back, feed and change her and continue driving. Unlike when the three of us made the trip together, I decided to stop after about twelve hours of driving and we spent the night in a hotel. She and I both like to do that. She loves cruising the hallways and going up and down on the elevators and getting something from the vending machine. (She doesn't seem to mind not being able to eat it.) We made it home and went back to our normal lives and loved going to the airport a few days later to pick up Mom.

***

In December of 2006, we attended the funeral for Uncle Bob whose noble struggle against ALS finally came to an end. The day we returned home from the funeral, Beth went off with an aide for a few hours and Merry noted in her journal: "I missed her while she was away. She adds so much

175

light and joy to our days when you look past the drudgery."
Amen. It is so true.

***

A couple of times a year, usually on Ash Wednesday and
Maundy Thursday, our church family gathers in our
Educational Building for a worship service following a
potluck supper. The Ash Wednesday service, particularly, is
not that well attended but always seems meaningful for those
who do make it. At some point, long before the advent of
video projectors and the high tech world of today, we used
overhead projectors to provide the words for praise choruses
or other songs not in our hymn book. We continue to use the
now archaic system for those two services because our video
projectors are quite securely fastened in the sanctuary and
youth room. Anyway, I mention that only because Beth
absolutely insists on being able to change the overheads for
the singing of the four or five numbers we will do during the
service. She can do the whole operation by herself, but loves
being able to choose someone to do it with her. For a week
or two before hand, at least five times or more a day, we will
hear her musing out loud, "Who can I pick to help me?" We
will offer suggestions to no avail. Often the person on whom
she has decided doesn't come and someone else has to be
drafted at the last minute. No matter, she will move ahead,
managing the work as if no one were there anyway, enjoying
being the center, or so she thinks, of everyone's attention.

And speaking of being the center of attention, there was
probably no time when she reveled in that more than during
the events surrounding her graduation from high school. She
had been sick a good bit that spring, for the first time in years,
and the last time for years afterwards. But she would turn

twenty-one (who would ever have thought it possible) that July, so the spring days of 2007 were her last days in the public school system. Though her last six or more years had been at Waynesburg in the special ed program there, she was graduating from Jefferson. We heard of and talked about nothing else but that graduation for weeks on end. Who was going to come see her graduate? How would she do it? Who was going to help her?

As it turned out, the evening went off beautifully. Four of her most special friends, Matt Blair (then the principal at Margaret Bell Miller), Blair Zimmerman (soon to become County Commissioner), Dave Calvario (then Director of the Bonner Program at Waynesburg University), and Randy Pettit (our next door chiropractor who visited with Beth almost every day) all came, just to see her. The always faithful Billie Jo escorted her onto her spot on the stage with the rest of the graduating class, but when her name was called she zoomed across the stage to receive her diploma (and far more importantly to her, a hug) from friend and fellow church member Bob Greenlee, representing the Jefferson Morgan School Board. The crowd that evening gave her quite an ovation. What a night.

And the Doreans, who are not known as the partying type, threw a veritable luau to celebrate this big event. More than a hundred of her favorite people filled our backyard to help us thank God for His goodness to us. Beth got so many hugs and exerted herself so much that she sort of crashed near the end of the affair and we had to take her inside to lie down. But not before she had seen Lucy the dog dressed in a grass skirt or heard her whole family doing a karaoke version of "Our Girl," with lyrics written just for her.

We had asked folks inclined to give a gift to instead donate money to an organization that makes manual wheelchairs out of PVC pipe for use in the third world and received almost $700.00 for their mission. (Beth got a whole lot of money and cards, and most importantly hugs, just for herself.)

***

Two weeks later her beloved Dennis Mattei died of colon cancer, which he had battled and, we thought and hoped, defeated years earlier. I had the privilege of doing Dennis' funeral service.

Two days later, I again had the privilege of doing another funeral, this one for our great friend, and for twenty-five years, the man who kept our cars on the road, George Kelley. Like so many, George, who could give the impression of being a tough nut but underneath had a heart of gold, had a very special place in his heart for Beth. Anytime work being done on one of our vans was for Beth, there would be no charge. Also an excellent woodworker, George was the one who took that old bath chair we had gotten years earlier from the Bruderhof and made a frame on wheels for it that served as her shower chair. Though neither Dennis nor George was what most folks would deem a religious man, (neither very often graced the doors of a church) the grace both men showed Beth and our family were, I believe, evidence of the grace they had received from Jesus.

***

And then on April 23, 2008, our family lost our dear friend, Stan Scott. Stan had been something of a second father to Merry and me and a grandfather for our girls. What a special man! We have never been sure how much of the whole dying process Beth understands at all. Mostly she just knows that folks she loves a lot are no longer around, folks whom she could always count on for a visit or a phone call, whose homes she could convince Dad to drop in on when out and about in the car, are suddenly no longer available. It takes Beth a while to process that these folks she has loved so much are now in heaven. For months after June Scott had died, Beth had asked Stan where June was. Eventually I think she got the idea that she was no longer with us but with God.

***

Beth has always had a remarkable eye for detail that I am sure we all have but, because of her limited mobility, she has really put to work. I have mentioned how she can tell us where stuff is in the house. In October of 2008, we went to a Waynesburg University football game. As at any event like that, her sole attention is on the people she can get to stop and talk with her. Well, here she spotted and latched onto for a long mid-game visit, her friend Randy Pettit, now out of the chiropractor business and working at Waynesburg University. Weeks later, she picked up one of those promotional magazines that they sell at sporting events that list all the players names and such. There on the back cover in a picture of the entire crowd at an earlier game, she spotted a minuscule Randy and was in seventh heaven pointing it out to anyone who would look.

***

A couple of weeks later, Beth and I did something we have done probably only a handful of times in her now thirty years. We went to see a movie in the theater, in this case, "High School Musical Three." We had been avid watchers of the first HSM movie. I can't tell you how many times she has watched it. We were not as thrilled with the second, but decided to take the plunge and watch the third one on the big screen.

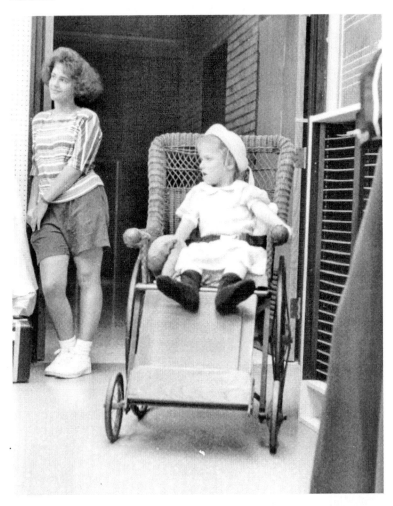

Those who frequent the theaters may not have an appreciation for the challenges involved in such an undertaking with Beth. Everyone deals with the cost factor, that's not an issue. More to the point is the sound levels; remember that she has a very low tolerance for loud noises. Then there is the problem of finding a movie that is age appropriate for a thirty year old who functions more on a first or second grade academic level and who is not enamored with any of the typical animated characters. Or there are issues where she just loses it because she is tired or scared or has just had a major blowout in her diapers and you have to find some place to change her somewhat discreetly. I am just saying.

Anyway, we took the plunge with HSM 3 and had a really good time. Mom dropped us off and spent her free time shopping at Target and Michaels and a few different places. Merry pretty much hates to shop, so it is never much fun going with her. She has her list of what she wants to get and is in and out before most of the rest of us are getting in the door. It has certainly been a blessing over the years because she almost never comes home with something she wasn't planning on getting: no impulse buying in that woman.

But for Beth and I who don't mind cruising the aisles, it is a challenge. So she had her idea of a shopping trip, and we hung out enjoying the story and the music of HSM 3.

Of course, it would never do for our family just to watch movies. We all have something of the would-be-actor in us and have through the years all taken part in a number of local productions. Four of us were in "The Sound of Music" together. Carrie and Hannah were in "The Wizard of Oz and even Beth had a cameo appearance as a "roll-on" in "The Music Man." I shouldn't have to tell you by now that she loved every minute of it.

***

On December 6 of that year, Beth and I shared a one-of-a-kind day. On that day Chris Hardie, who was at the time working with me on the County of Greene

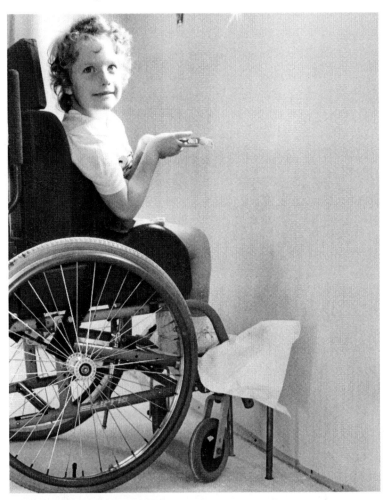

Redevelopment Authority, did one of his incredibly long runs. For several years, Chris had crisscrossed the county on increasingly long runs to raise money for the American Cancer Society. Chris and I served together on the Board of

Greene County Habitat, and he decided to do a fund raiser for Habitat.

The plan was for him to run to all fifty homes the organization had built or rehabbed and sold to folks in need since its inception in 1984. Since I was one of the few folks who had a clue where all fifty homes were positioned throughout the county and knew most, if not all, of the homeowners, I got drafted, along with our photographer for the day, Damon Neroni, to set out with Chris at about 6:00 A.M. The idea was that he would run from house to house, posing for a photo with each family. Needless to say, it was cold and very dark when we set out.

Chris was in remarkable shape and took off through those early morning hours while Damon and I drove along beside or behind him with caution lights flashing to offer some protection. At some point, I felt like he was getting a bit weary, and so I jumped out and ran with him. We were joined in the run between Crucible and Clarksville as we ran along the Greene River Trail by a couple of his running buddies. When we parted company with them, I just kept on going.

When we got to Jefferson, we stopped off at our house for some food and drink, and Beth pressed to join us. By that point, Damon had headed home and the support car was being driven by Chris' wife, Kelley, and a good friend. I sheepishly asked if they would consider hauling Beth for a few miles with them, and they enthusiastically agreed. We arranged to have Merry pick her up in a few miles, but had to call her off because the three of them had so much fun together that she ended up going the whole way to West Waynesburg with them.

Every time we would pause from running to get some water or a snack, Chris and I found the three of them laughing hilariously about something. Chris ended up logging something more than thirty miles and I put in just about half of that amount. I don't know how far Beth rode in the car, but she definitely won the award for having the most fun.

***

A week later she appeared in that year's Christmas program at church as (what else?) a star. I think she has been an angel or a star every year we have done a production. She absolutely loves getting fitted for her costume, loves being in all the rehearsals, insists on a copy of the manuscript so that she can help Mom or Dad or whoever is directing the show that year. She lives and breathes the play and always, always, always freezes up and has to be coached through whatever tiny part she has. Go figure.

***

CHAPTER EIGHTEEN

And On Life Goes 2009 and Beyond

MERRY NOTES IN her journal entry of June 17 that Charlie Anderson says that Beth has taught him to say, "I love you," and not just to her. Charlie is a wonderful friend to our whole family. He has traveled to D.C. with me to help build a fence for Carrie and Ryan's yard. And in the last five years, Merry calls him more often than me when she needs a project done. He is a great student of the Bible and teaches one of our kids' Sunday school classes. He is one of the most generous people I know, with his time and his money. But for all of that, maybe because of the way he was brought up, he has had a very difficult time saying, "I love you."

Enter Beth, who can drive me nuts at times by saying, "Love you, Dad," dozens of times an hour as we are driving along in the car and there is nothing to distract her. She calls Charlie just about every morning of the week, and somewhere in the conversation, you will hear, "I love you, Charlie." The good Lord continues to use her in all of our lives in ways one would never expect.

***

That summer we gathered with a large number of Merry's relatives at her family's preferred getaway spot, Lake Wallenpaupac in the Poconos in eastern Pennsylvania. The house the family rented for the week was on a steep hillside which made getting Beth down to the water a challenge. Beth did not swim that summer, but loved sitting in a chair or lying on the dock with her family all about her. God bless the family!

When Beth gets especially playful she gets kind of bossy, telling anyone around what they should be doing to keep the party going. So there she was on the dock, ordering this person to dive and that person to jump and someone else to sit and talk with her and, well, you get the picture. Everyone was scurrying about doing whatever she ordered them to do, which only egged her on to do more and more of it, while she and everyone around her were dying of laughter.

***

On September 4, 2009, we traveled to eastern Ohio to be a part of a wedding for Laura Ellis and Andrew Hartle. Laura had done a lot of care for Beth over her four years at Waynesburg University and while worshipping at JBC. Her parents, Chuck and Sally, had been friends of ours from twenty-five years ago when they had worked with the Coalition for Christian Outreach at Waynesburg. I was to do the service for Laura and Andrew and the Ellises invited us to stay in a beautiful lake house that had been built for her parents as their health declined and so was remarkably accessible.

Beth loved this time with them. Not only did she get hugs from Chuck and Andrew and any other good looking man around, but Sally talked to her, almost as an adult to adult, something very, very few people ever do, her parents included. In typical Beth fashion, she wanted something to do to help out. So the morning of the wedding we stuffed candy favors for all the guests. It was the perfect task for Beth, doing the same simple task over and over and over again. She was not happy when we had to leave the festivities early to make the three hour drive home so that dad could be ready to preach the next morning.

***

That Thanksgiving we welcomed my sister, Cathy, and her family from Wooster, Ohio for Thanksgiving. Craig and Hannah were also in. So what else do you do with such a crowd? You go kayaking. We rounded up eight kayaks, including a double one for me and Beth. Our nephew, Sam, now a doctor of physical therapy, actually tipped his kayak looking back at his dad and had to drive home to get some dry clothes on. They were just in for the day and had not brought a change of clothes so he ended up raiding my bureau. He and his dad made fun of the jeans and t-shirt he came back in as being more than a little out of fashion, but I thought he looked pretty good in them. Beth who begs to be a part of such an outing, did OK for about half an hour before becoming terribly uncomfortable and having a bit of a meltdown.

In May of 2011, while visiting our good friend and physician assistant, Shannon Scango (now Wilkins) we witnessed one of God's little miracles. Shannon has a wonderful golden retriever named Mattie. She is friendly without totally knocking you down and loves to play ball, something I did with her most times we were together. Well, guess who wanted to get in on that action? So everyone else who plays ball with Mattie has to wrestle the ball from her jaws. Or occasionally she will drop the ball at some distance from you. But with Beth, who could not throw the ball more than a yard or two at most (and who, obviously, did not begin to have the strength to tug the ball away from her), Mattie

would bring the ball and gently lay it in her lap. Shannon assured us she had never done that for anyone else. It was as if she somehow understood that here was a person who needed special treatment and provided it for her. To this day, it blows my mind.

On May 3 of 2011, local piano teacher and friend, Carol Silbaugh, offered to give Beth free piano lessons. If you could see Beth's weak and crooked fingers trying to play the piano, well, it is a sight. But she slowly learned to pick out the notes, learned to read music. A week after her first lesson, Beth drove around the house for an hour with her piano book in hand, waiting for Carol. They went on for several years, Carol showing exceptional care and thoughtfulness. She insisted that Beth be a part of her annual recital and patiently encouraged her when she went into still another of her freezing in front of people routines. Like Sally Ellis, she treated Beth with a dignity and respect that most of us don't muster.

A week after her second lesson, Beth fell off the lift of the van at Pathways, the adult day care program she went to once a week for a number of years. We got a call from the program director and that was all she told us. We could only imagine: a four hundred pound chair falling four feet with a kid strapped inside. Head and neck injuries seemed a given. We flew to the local hospital thinking she might be dead. We are about eight miles from the hospital, the center is about one mile. We beat them there. When we didn't see them when we walked in the emergency room doors, our hearts totally flipped. Are they trying to resuscitate her? Did they take her directly to one of the larger hospitals? What's going on? It turned out that the Pathways folks had to get every other kid off of the bus and make provisions for them and then reload Beth. She rolled into the hospital with barely a cut or bruise. She had backed out of the van onto an already partially lowered lift. The cushioning of the chair itself (and the grace of God) apparently protected her. So after a series of x-rays and CAT scans, she was pronounced good to go.

***

The following Christmas, most of the family was in town and we got a good old-fashioned Pennsylvania snow storm. The grandkids were between the ages of ten and two and most had never seen anything like it. So we dragged out the old family sleds that our girls had used when they were younger and one that I had used when I was a kid and rounded up some plastic ones and a couple of round disks and headed out to the elementary school to do some sled-riding. For one who had grown up sledding down the really steep hill at the end of the parks in Waynesburg, the gentle slope at the school was embarrassingly tame. But we all had a ball.

I had taken Beth sled-riding up at our property on Haver's Hill years before. But she got cold and wet and miserable very quickly. With seven grandkids to keep entertained, I was not up for adding on trying to keep Beth happy, so she drove out with one of the girls and watched the action out the window of the car, warm, dry and once again enjoying being the boss and telling us all what to do.

***

On September 4, 2013 Beth had the first of what has become something of a recurring issue. She and Merry were at the local orthotics center getting fitted for a new brace when she had a...well, she had something. Her reaction mimicked the kind of pain that she had first experienced with the onset of the pulmonary embolisms just a few days before her lung was removed. Thinking that that might be the case again, Merry called for an ambulance. By the time the EMT folks arrived on the scene she was fine, joking with Merry and the orthotics staff. The ambulance staff checked her out and left. Merry and Beth came home and all seemed well.

Then after nap that same afternoon, it happened again, this time so severely that Merry again called for the ambulance and this time Beth was life-flighted to Presbyterian Hospital in Pittsburgh. There she was put on an IV drip, had blood work, a CAT scan of her lungs and a whole lot of attention. Hannah and Craig rushed to the hospital. Away for most of the day, I was the last to arrive. And there was Beth, chatting away with Craig and the other medical professionals like it was a college reunion.

So what was it? We are left thinking that she has severe muscle spasms, a pinched nerve or something similar. She can go months without them but will sometimes have several episodes in a week's period. Sometimes they seem mild and pass quickly. Other times they are dramatic: she will turn white, drool, and once, she actually passed out for a second or two. It is obvious that she is in great pain and frustrating that we don't know what to do to help her. Given that severe curvature of her spine, in many ways it is quite remarkable that such things don't happen a great deal more often. We try to get her a massage once a month or so (good friend, Jaime Bedillion Wood has volunteered to come once a month to our house to give Beth, and often times Merry, some relief from their aches and pains) to try to help with it and we continue to pursue ideas, with the occasional test, to try to figure out what is happening and how we can help.

***

In September of 2014, we were totally thrilled to have Brittany Morrison, a long time friend of Hannah and one of the brightest spirits around, become an aide to Beth for one day a week. Her regular aide, Tammy Roberts, (one of Beth's all time favorite people who has for years now taken her to a Christian adult day care program, 2nd Sam 9, shopping at Walmart and Giant Eagle, roller-skating in Greensboro and entertained her for hours doing crafts at home) only wanted to work four days a week and did not like to take Beth to the Wellness Center to swim. Tammy helped train Brit on Beth's care needs. And Brit has had her own life's challenges with a daughter who has successfully battled cancer and a young son with autism.

All of that just to say she was uniquely prepared to handle working with Beth. But on her first solo day with Beth, she allowed Beth to talk her out of going swimming. Welcome to our world. The kid is, maybe we all are, downright manipulative, complaining of aches and pains, whining about how she doesn't want to do something, and those new to her care, already feeling sorry for her for her condition, tend to give in to her. With a little encouragement from Beth's parents, Brit has been a model of redirecting those negatives complaints.

A couple of weeks later, Merry, Beth and I took off for our first of its kind vacation, all by ourselves. We went to the family's favorite stomping grounds, Cape May for three days, staying in a hotel rather than the usual rented house. As mentioned, motels/hotels are not Merry's favorite place to spend a night, so she gamely endured our time. Beth and I loved it. There were both an outdoor pool where I swam laps each day and an indoor pool where we hung out when the weather got rainy. But we walked the board walk, much less crowded with the summer crowd gone, and ate out every meal, something Merry and I enjoyed and Beth put up with. I swore we would do it every fall, but so far we have not repeated the trip.

***

One thing we have discovered over the years is that Beth can enjoy watching a TV show or movie over and over again. She does that with her iPad almost every afternoon. When they first wake from the daily nap, Merry lets Beth stay on her Bi-pap for a while, during which time she watches YouTube or Netflix or some other video, and often watches the same ones over and over again. Nowhere is that more true than watching brief snippets of her niece Clara on Merry's iPhone. I can watch a particularly fun one maybe two or three times, and then I am done. But Beth can lie there for half an hour watching the same one multiple times, saying with each repetition, "Dad, you've gotta watch this."

***

Birthdays have become an increasingly big deal for Beth as the years go by. We had the big party for year number twenty-one that coincided with graduation from high school and thought that we were good till thirty. But about six months before her twenty-ninth birthday, she started talking about it. And when I say she talked about it, I mean it was a topic of her conversation every day, multiple times a day.

When the big day arrived, she actually woke up and the first words out of her mouth were, "This is my big day! I'm twenty-nine." For a day that her parents were not putting much into, it turned out to be a pretty big deal. She got multiple phone calls from all of her favorites (that included Randy and Mike and Dr. Martha). Ty Cole brought her flowers (yikes, he put her dad to shame). Charlie Anderson brought her two videos and she raked in over $200.00 in cards that either came in the mail or that accompanied a personal visit. My birthday is on May 29 in case anyone cares.

But the celebration of number twenty-nine was all unplanned. That was not the case for year number thirty. We began talking about it early on. Emily wanted to bring her five kids in to let them experience a Vacation Bible School at Jefferson Baptist the way she had all her years of growing up. They decided that was more of a priority for them than the yearly family trip to Cape May so the rest of the family came on board. Carrie (and later in the week Ryan) and the girls also came up. Craig and a very pregnant Hannah and Clara who were packing for their move to Colorado in July (another reason the beach trip got canceled) came down and we threw Beth a thirtieth birthday party to remember. A good friend, Pete Arigoni, arranged to get us the huge popcorn popper from the Fire Hall, and spent the afternoon popping and bagging popcorn. Brittany made some very special cupcakes for the occasion. Carrie set up a photo booth where folks could dress up in crazy costumes and get their pictures taken. Ryan and Matt agreed to fry funnel cakes with equipment we borrowed from Jon and Jennifer Wolfe. And more than a hundred (we should have had a guest registry set up but didn't) of her most favorite people in the world stopped by to wish her a happy birthday.

The party spread out over the whole grounds of the church and parsonage. At one point we invited everyone to come inside to sing "Happy Birthday."

In typical Beth fashion, she chose the very minute I was speaking, about how grateful we were for everyone's coming and for the enormous gift of love that all of these wonderful people had given to Beth over her life time, to leave the building. I will never know whether it was because she was embarrassed or emotionally unsure about how to handle it or whether it was because she was, like the rest of her family, a real ham who left so as to be able to turn around and make a grand entry. It was a great day.

***

This past fall of 2016, Merry, Beth and I made a trip out west to visit our family in CO and OK. Hannah was preparing to give birth to her second child and Merry has missed only one delivery of our now nine grandchildren. The plan had been to go to OK to see Em and Matt and their five for a couple of days and then go on to CO to be there for the birth. But even as we were driving west, Hannah called to say that she had had some major contractions the night before and so maybe we should rework our plans.

So when we hit St. Louis, instead of heading southwest on I44 towards OK, we stayed on I70 for CO.

It turned out that Hannah didn't deliver Miles for another week, but we had a wonderful time, seeing their new home, worshipping with their new church family, seeing the sights, hiking, running, swimming and mostly loving on our precious two year old Clara.

But for Beth, even that wonderful time was severely limited by her inability to breathe at the eight thousand foot elevation of Buena Vista. We knew from our previous visits that she would need to be on oxygen the entire time, so, even before we got to Colorado Springs in the eastern part of the state, we had put her on two liters of O2. But we had not done a good job of getting a face apparatus that would work well for her. Our previous time there she had worn a big mask that, while comfortable for breathing, really distanced her from people. So we thought a nasal cannula would work best. But the one we had rubbed her nose wrong and a device we picked up at a local hospital supply outfit was even more uncomfortable. So the poor kid was uncomfortable most of the ten days we were in CO.

Obviously, she couldn't hike any trails with us, and her 02 levels were compromised anytime we went much above eight thousand feet, so she/we were limited in what we could do. But hanging with our family was all we really wanted to do anyway.

Beth could not wait to get to the hospital to "help Hannah" when she heard the baby was born, and loved being near him when we brought him home. She loves babies.

***

In the days of editing this work, I had the pleasure of having breakfast with good friend, Larry Hagyari. Larry and his wife, Linda, have been stalwart members and participants at JBC for decades. But as they have been adapting to retired life, they have grown a little slack in their attendance. Larry said he knew that they needed to get back into a regular habit of worship. And he said confessionally, "You know one of the things I miss most about worship is seeing Beth and getting hugs from her." And then he added with a deep chuckle, "She always kept me on time." I puzzled over that for a minute before realizing what he meant.

Always the enthusiastic greeter, Beth most often calls out in the loudest voice, a huge smile on her face and her arms spread wide for a hug, "Larry Hagyari!" That's nice if you are on time and OK if the congregation is singing a hymn. But if she bellows out your name in the middle of a prayer or announcement or some such quiet moment, well, everyone in church is going to smile knowing exactly who just got busted for being late. Beth, of course, doesn't have a clue that that's what's happening. She's just greeting a friend.

***

EPILOGUE

Where does one end this story? As the last section makes clear, stories and adventures with Beth continue every day. Normally, I suppose, a book like this is written at the end of someone's life. But what once seemed a total pipe dream, daily becomes more and more a likely possibility: that Beth will outlive Merry and me.

The girl who wasn't supposed to last six months at most is now thirty and a half and going stronger than ever. She is, quite frankly, and has been for years now, at least in all the normal kind of ways, healthier than either Merry or I am. Yeah, she does get an occasional cold, sometimes has an upset stomach, and is often plagued by pretty severe menstrual cramps. But her colds seem to last only a day or two. And she does not have the deteriorating eye sight, the aches and pains of old age, the likelihood that our best days are way behind us that Merry and I face.

So we come to this stage in our life, a year or two out from probable retirement, with Beth very much still a part of our lives, and no indications that that is going to change anytime soon. True, she only has one lung, true she is already six years past what one of the best doctors in the world considered her maximum life expectancy. So she could go in a heartbeat. But then so could either of us.

We had never in our wildest dreams considered that we would still be caring for her in retirement. All of our dreaming about what we might do, where we might go was as a duo, not a trio. Merry and I used to talk about the possibility of buying an RV, and spending the years rotating every four months of the year parked near one of the kids' families.

But you can't live in an RV with a kid in a wheelchair, at least not with a kid in a wheelchair who is as full of energy as Beth. She would go nuts, and so would we.

So our kids talk about us living near one of them so that they and their kids can be a part of caring for Beth as we grow older and more frail. Of course, there have been conversations, always painful, about who would, who will take over Beth's care if Merry and I die or become unable to care for her any longer.

I don't want anyone to think that we are cold and heartless and longing for our kid to die. Nothing would be farther from the truth. We love Bethany with everything inside of us and would, will do anything in our power and ability to care for her. She so totally enriches our lives and blesses our hearts. Losing her would be a devastating blow for our whole family, even though we would at the same time rejoice that her spirit would at last be set free to run and play amidst the mountains and plains of heaven. But only in the last few years has it begun to dawn us that she may well be among those who mourn our passing instead of the other way around.

So I choose to write her story, incomplete as it is, now, rather than not being able to write it when death finally relieves her of the burden of her weakened body.

She has changed our lives for the good forever, and is still doing so. Her wry smiles and willingness to laugh at any silly thing that happens or is said fill us with such incredible joy. Merry and I both wish that we had more energy to invest in her, more patience with her difficult moments, but we live with no regrets about the life that God has given us with Beth.

It is a fair question to ask, what about all of those prayers, ours and thousands of others, that God would heal her? Were they answered? Well, certainly not as we had hoped and maybe even expected in those first days of her life when we gathered as her family with her church family and laid the desires of our hearts before the Lord.

Prayer remains something of a mystery to me, in large measure because of our experiences with Beth. I am infinitely more confident in the goodness of God today than I was thirty years ago because I see the incredible goodness her life has brought to so many.

I have not a single doubt that I am a better man than I would have been without these thirty years with Beth. What do I mean by that? Simply this: there has not been the time or energy to indulge my ego about being president of the United States or a famous pastor or the dad of some star athlete or scholar or any of the other vain foolishness that used to swell my soul with arrogant pride. I am humbler, more caring, more focused on others' needs than I would ever have been without her.

I also have not a single doubt that we are a better family than we would have been without these years with Beth. Our girls and their husbands and their children are all remarkable people of whom we are enormously proud and who love Jesus in a way that causes us to weep with thanksgiving. But that is in large measure because the years with Beth have forced us to focus on what matters most in life: loving God, loving other people, being agents of the Kingdom. And, while the girls and their families have certainly experienced material success and done some really cool things with their lives, none of them have lost track of all those life lessons that

Beth's life has brought to us all.

And, I would also say our church family is incredibly better off today than we would have been without Beth. Oh sure, if you look, just about every doorway and wall have marks where Beth has banged her chair, despite her remarkable skills with it. But the caring spirit that has grown up over these thirty years that was first directed at her and her family has become a mark of who we are as a church family that most visitors notice right away.

Much of that goodness would never have happened had God swept down in those early days and performed a miracle of the kind we most definitely wanted Him to perform. So no, I would have to say that God did not answer our prayers, not the way we prayed them. But part of what makes Him God is that He is sovereign and knows better than we what is best for us.

In giving us Beth the way she is, rather than the way we thought we wanted her, God has answered our prayer far more beautifully, far more completely than we could have begun to imagine those long years ago.

Her life is each and every day a testament to the promises of God to never leave us or forsake us. That such a frail being could so totally enrich the lives of many, who have much more of the "normal" physical and mental giftedness, is a reminder that, indeed, the secret things belong to God. Our kids and grandkids, our family and friends (many of whom deserve but did not get even a mention in this book) need to know and remember her story so that God may receive the glory that is due Him for His sustaining presence in Beth's life, and all of ours as well.

John Rich Dorean
January 2017